||| ||| ||| ||||| |||| || ||| |||| |||
SO-BZE-386

92

B
ZENGER Galt, Tom
Peter Zenger, fighter
for freedom

Date Due

11-27-67			
10/14/70			
Jan 5			

Brought to trial in 1735 for printing unpopular information, Zenger, with Alexander
Hamilton as his lawyer, won this important
case for freedom of the press in America.

Wm. Davies School Library

Wm. Davies School Library
Jenckes Hill Rd., Lincoln, RI

DEMCO

Peter Zenger

FIGHTER FOR FREEDOM

BOOKS BY TOM GALT

Seven Days from Sunday
Peter Zenger: Fighter for Freedom
How the United Nations Works
Volcano

Peter Zenger

FIGHTER FOR FREEDOM

BY TOM GALT

ILLUSTRATED BY RALPH RAY

NEW YORK: THOMAS Y. CROWELL COMPANY

Copyright 1951 by Tom Galt

All rights reserved. No part of this book may be reproduced in any form, except by a reviewer, without the permission of the publisher

Designed by Maurice Serle Kaplan

Manufactured in the United States of America by the Vail-Ballou Press, Inc., Binghamton, New York

EIGHTH PRINTING

Contents

CONTENTS

"The trial of Zenger in 1735 was the germ of American freedom, the morning star of that liberty which subsequently revolutionized America."—GOUVERNEUR MORRIS.

*   *   *

"The famous case of Peter Zenger established the law of New York in favor of freedom of the press and established for all time the principle of the liberty of the press in America."—*History of the Bench and Bar of New York,* edited by the HON. DAVID MCADAM.

*   *   *

"The case of Zenger of New York was a popular cause. The liberty of the press depended on it."—BENJAMIN FRANKLIN's *Pennsylvania Gazette* for December 1, 1737.

Peter Zenger

FIGHTER FOR FREEDOM

CHAPTER ONE

The Immigrants

UNDER the flapping sails and creaking ropes the silent men, women, and children stood crowded together on the deck of the wooden ship.

Peter, a tall, thin boy of thirteen, shaded his eyes from the summer sun and gazed across the bay. He felt the challenge of the little town of blue-roofed, red-brick houses huddled on that unfamiliar shore.

Heavy and gray, straight in front of them, an old fort caught the sunlight on its long, grim walls. Beside it stood a gallows ready to hang someone. And over the warehouses the sharp-pointed steeples of New York's half-dozen churches reached high into the sky.

Peter drew a long breath, shaken with the excitement of arriving. Catching his younger brother under the arms, he raised him up where he could see between the heads of the other passengers. "Look, John. That's where we're going to live." He added, laughing, "See the flying machine! They tie a rope round your neck, and up you go in the air!"

The boys' attention was caught by the one little boat that came out to welcome them, an Indian-style canoe. A strong, well-built Negro was paddling. With him rode the city's one official who inspected all incoming ships and collected the mail. He was a round, self-important little man with a large moustache and fat cheeks, sweating this June day in a long brown coat with huge cuffs.

Climbing up a rope ladder onto the ship, he took one look around, coughed, and held his nose. For two and a half months on the ocean all these people had been hungry and thirsty, as there had not been enough food or water for so many. The ship was so crowded that the passengers could not all come up on deck at once; there was not enough space.

The captain explained glumly, "We set sail with close to three hundred aboard. Now there are only two hundred and seventy."

"What took off the others?" asked the official.

"Fevers, I guess. Since there's no doctor aboard, how should I know? The Queen paid for their passage, and here they are. Take 'em ashore!"

Peter's father and mother, driven from their homes in Germany by a war with the French, had been hiding in the Black Forest when he was born. A few years later they had fled for their lives again from swarms of both French and German soldiers who would have killed them because of their Protestant religious beliefs. For five years they and many thousands of their neighbors from the Lower Palatinate on the Rhine worked farms in the Netherlands. But King Louis XIV, the tyrant of France, lashed out again with his armies, burning houses and crops, and they all nearly starved, till Queen Anne sent a fleet of ships to Rotterdam and carried thirty thousand refugees to England.

But some could find no jobs there. After two years the government offered many of them free passage to America and promised to lend them money if they would tap the pine forests to make tar and turpentine for English ships.

The Zenger family set sail eagerly, hoping to find peace after so many years of trouble—to carve out a farm of their own in the free new world and earn a good living selling those supplies to the navy. But fever broke out in the cabins on the way, and Peter saw his father die on the high seas.

Though Peter was thirteen years old and strong for his age, what could he and his widowed mother do to earn a living for themselves and his younger brother and sister in this unknown town with the grim, gray fort and the gallows ready to hang a man?

3

When at last the crowded ship was tied at a stone wharf, the official announced in a loud voice, "Those who can walk, can go ashore. Those who can't walk, must stay on board till they get well or—" He shrugged and climbed hurriedly down the ladder.

He led them through the streets. The long, ragged procession staggered behind him, carrying their bundles. The smells from the gutters and from the houses seemed especially strong and sour after so many weeks on the ocean. New York was small compared with the European cities Peter had seen. In ten minutes they walked all the way through its dirty streets and out onto an open field, the Common, where rows of mildewed white tents awaited them.

Here they found their companions, the other Palatines who had sailed from England about the same time they had. But not all were here. Some thirty-four hundred had left England. Now there were scarcely three thousand. Peter could see that very soon there would be fewer. Typhus was so common among them, it was called "Palatine fever" that summer.

The tent city had been divided into six companies, each with its own captain in command. The little Zenger family was greeted by a Palatine man whom they had known in the Netherlands and in England. He assigned them to a tent with four other families and gave them a few coins, a loan from the government.

4

That evening, while his mother was busy with the other women in front of the tent cooking a little supper, Peter sat with the men talking inside. Noticing four books lying on a little chest near a sick man, he went to look at them and opened their badly worn covers one by one. Often in the last few years he had wished he could read better. But in his wandering life he had never been to a school and had seldom held a book in his hands.

The sick man asked, "Did your father teach you your ABC's?"

Peter hesitated. "Once in Rotterdam he borrowed a book in the Dutch language and taught me a little. I wanted to learn more."

"Take this, and see if you can understand it." The man raised himself painfully on one elbow and picked out one of the volumes. "It's a geography, written in Dutch. Here's a chapter on America. Begin with this."

After supper, in the light of the long summer evening, Peter lay outside on his stomach on the cool-smelling grass with the book. Slowly, as he read, he forgot his worry about how he could earn a living in this unknown place. Although some of the words were too difficult, he succeeded in spelling out a page and a half describing this new country, this America.

A tingle of pleasure went through him from having

the land opened up to his mind by the lines of print. He could see the hundreds of miles of forests and prairies, with bears and wolves, and the Indians' tents. Somehow he must—he promised himself this—he must learn to read better.

Books seemed very wonderful things. Surely great honor must go to the men who wrote them and who printed them. For a moment he even pictured himself making a book and being congratulated by all his neighbors.

Meanwhile the men around him were discussing the governor's proclamation to keep down the price of food. They evidently liked the new governor.

As Peter did not understand much about politics, he raised his head with surprise when a thin, unshaven German carpenter, who had been here two months, laughed and told the others, "No, far from it! Not all the governors are good! Why, the last one here they put in jail."

Peter protested, "But the people can't put their governor in jail!"

"They did it here," the man assured him, killing a mosquito that had landed on his bare arm. "And his Excellency would still be in the pen if he hadn't bribed the sheriff to let him out."

The carpenter turned and pointed, still holding the

7

mosquito between first finger and thumb. "Right there. The jail is on the ground floor, to the right of the entrance."

The others moved their heads all at the same time. A muddy lane led into the town to where the City Hall, a heavy brick building, stood squarely across the street. As they looked, a candle was lighted in one of the windows where the prison was.

Peter pictured a royal governor all dressed up in fancy silks, with haughty servants waiting on him. The idea of such a personage being locked in that little place seemed so ridiculous that Peter laughed.

He did not think that he himself might some day be locked in that same jail.

CHAPTER TWO

Peter Sees a Job

PETER ran through the little town with his younger
brother in search of fun.

Stopping in front of a shoemaker's shop, the boys
looked down at their broken boots. Peter wiggled the
toe that stuck out through a hole.

"Mister Apprentice," he said to a young man busily
nailing on a heel at a bench near the open door, "will
you mend my shoes if I sing you a funny song?"

But the master rose from his seat further inside the
shop and scolded, "Be off with ye!"

As they ran on toward the water front, Peter's mind
began to work on an idea. It seemed the only solution
to the great problem of how he was ever going to earn
a living here. After a minute he stopped suddenly.
"John," he exclaimed, "I wish I could be an apprentice!
It's the only way to learn a trade."

9

Now they could see the masts of the ships over the house roofs, but a loud squeaking in another shop attracted their attention. They went to the open doorway to watch.

A young man was working a big wooden machine, a sort of table on which heavy wooden braces at each side supported a huge wooden screw six inches thick standing straight up in the middle.

The husky young man turned the screw, raising a flat piece like a lid attached to the bottom of it. He pulled out a sheet of paper from between this flat piece and the table, slipped in another paper, and pressed the flat lid down again by pushing a long lever stuck in the upper end of the screw. He grunted and sweated, heaving on that lever as hard as he could.

"What is it?" John asked.

"I saw one in the Netherlands," Peter answered. "It works like this: you're the paper, and I'm the press." Placing his left hand heavily on John's head, he grabbed an imaginary lever in the air with his right hand. He walked around his brother, pretending to push the lever very hard, grunting with the effort and making loud squeals in imitation of the noisy machine. Meanwhile his left hand pushed John's head lower and lower toward the unpaved muddy street.

"All done!" shouted John, on his knees. "I'm all printed now!"

The master of the shop came to the door, a dignified gentleman, looking serious. "Be off!" he commanded. "Have you nothing more profitable to do than to make noise in the street?"

He glared with shrewd little eyes, which Peter did not quite like. His heavy shoulders and strong barrel chest seemed stuffed into his many-buttoned waistcoat and white shirt with the sleeves rolled up. He tried to brush the sweat from his protruding forehead with the back of one hand, for his fingers were covered with black ink.

"I'm a printer," Peter announced.

"And I'm the paper," John, kneeling in the street, explained. "Don't you want me to be a book?"

"Like that one," Peter added, pointing to the sign he had just noticed. Hanging over the door, a board swung slowly in the wind, painted to look like a Bible.

"You're a brawny lad, at that," the gentleman admitted, narrowing his sharp eyes thoughtfully and looking hard at Peter. "How old are you?"

Peter tried to wipe the smile off his face respectfully. "Thirteen, sir."

"Is that all? You're big for your age. Can you read and write English?"

"No, sir."

The gentleman turned away, the tail of his wig bobbing about with annoyance.

11

Peter quickly added, "I can read and write a little in Dutch, sir, and I'd like to work at the Sign of the Bible, sir."

The old gentleman seemed pleased, for he looked back. "Where did you learn Dutch?"

"In Rotterdam, sir. I was born in Germany, but I lived a long time in the Netherlands, then a couple of years in England before we came here." Peter hoped his knowledge of languages would help him. "I don't know if you print any books in Dutch—"

"Yes, we do," the man snapped. "But who will pay your apprentice fee? Can your father spare fifteen shillings?"

Peter looked down at the muddy ruts under his feet in embarrassment. "My father died on shipboard on our way here." He knew that if his mother had that much money, she needed it for food. For him somehow to get such a sum (about fifteen dollars in modern money) was out of the question.

The man sighed with disappointment. "Well, run along now. There's too much work to be done in New York for sturdy boys to stand about idling."

As Peter walked slowly away he did not cry. It was not a time for tears or excitement. This was only the fate he had really expected all along. He could not learn a trade and earn a good living. He would have to sell himself as a bond servant and be a laborer all his life, chopping wood, carrying water, driving a cart for starvation wages, dressed in rags all his life long, digging ditches, digging graves.

CHAPTER THREE

Peter's Life Work Is Decided

THE good citizens of New York became alarmed at having so many sick people in tents on their Common north of Wall Street, for typhoid soon spread through the town like a terrifying ghost, strangling a man here, a child there.

So the Palatines were all sent to Nutten Island (later called Governor's Island), where they built huts for themselves.

The men were soon very busy moving again, for as Governor Hunter wrote to the officials in London:

The poor Palatines have been mighty sickly but are rapidly recovering. We have lost over 470 of our number.

I have been obliged to purchase 6,000 acres for them on Hudson's River about 100 miles up, where they are to be planted in five villages on both sides of the river. I am making all possible haste to send them before the winter.

Peter stood sorrowfully behind the group of men near the largest hut on Nutten Island. The men were eagerly discussing plots of land with the governor's agent, George Clarke, a slow, careful businessman, who sat at a table covered with papers. Any immigrant who agreed to take a plot, had to sign a promise to build a house, clear a field and plant it, make a certain amount of tar or turpentine from the trees near by, and pay all the taxes and fees within two years. The printed agreement also said, "The children from eight years and upwards are to be usefully employed to help the adults by gathering wood and boiling pitch and rosin."

But no one would offer land to a thirteen-year-old boy. Every day boatloads of families set off up the Hudson. And every day Peter was one of the friends left waving good-bye on the island. August wore into September. Peter, shivering, tore down an empty hut for firewood.

By the middle of October, among the deserted, crude buildings on Nutton Island, only two or three still sheltered a few widows and orphans.

Peter as usual went with the other children to the main building, but the governor's agent sat alone at his table, packing away his papers. Peter stood and watched.

Mr. Clarke looked up at the children and drummed his fingers on the table. "And now what are we going to do with you?" He stood up, gathering his papers

15

under his arm, and looked at Peter. "Would you like to be apprenticed to a trade?"

"Yes!" Peter answered loudly. But he added uneasily, "Who will pay my fee?"

The deputy secretary frowned. "Oh, so that's the problem, is it? I must speak to the governor. The women will have to become servants or get jobs in taverns or shops. But the children— Well, we shall see." He marched off heavily to the canoe that awaited him.

A week later, on a frosty morning, Peter looked up from chopping firewood and saw a husky young man in a fine warm coat striding boldly up the path between the huts. Peter recognized the printer's son, whose name he had found out by asking questions, and ran eagerly to meet him. "Good morning, Mr. Bradford!"

The young gentleman smiled just a little. "So you know my name! Well, now show me the strongest lad on this island, and I'll give you a penny."

"You can keep your penny, sir. You have found him for yourself."

Peter noticed that Andrew Bradford quickly put his penny back in his pocket and buttoned the flap over it. Wasting no time, he demanded, "Where's your mother?"

Peter led his mother out of their hut. He knew better than to invite a gentleman's son into such a miserable home.

16

Again Andrew Bradford came to the point without wasting any words. "Will you consent to have your son apprenticed to my father, the Printer to the King?"

"Printer to the King!" she exclaimed, fumbling nervously at her ragged shawl. She looked as startled as though she were being asked to consent to let her son become a prince. When she turned to Peter to learn his opinion, he was nodding his head so hard that some of his hair hit him in the eye.

"Why—yes," she stammered. "Yes, of course! But—?"

"Then I'll ask you both to come with me to sign the indenture," young Bradford concluded and marched off, leading the way.

Peter was speechless. In his excitement he trotted along with his mouth open, shifting his knitted wool cap back and forth, back and forth, from one hand to the other. At last he blurted out, "Then I don't have to pay any fee?"

"Oh, that!" sniffed the printer's son. "Governor Hunter persuaded the Council to apprentice the orphans of the Palatines; so the government will pay the fees. Come along."

The government? What was that? Peter shrugged. Well, he thought, three cheers for the government! I hope we'll always have such a friendly one!

CHAPTER FOUR

The Apprentice

PETER ZENGER learned to love the busy, smelly shop before he found out the dangers hidden there. Soon he noticed that his master's face sometimes looked tightly drawn or tired even in the middle of the morning. But the good-natured young apprentice did not pay much attention to that. He had his own exploring to do in his marvelous new craft.

Mr. Bradford's home was an old Dutch house built when the city had still been called New Amsterdam. From the doorway Peter could see the Old Market on a wharf and the ships' masts over the housetops and smell the salt air and the tarred ropes.

Entering the front door, under the slowly swinging sign of the Bible, he walked directly into the workroom with its two presses, run by Andrew Bradford and the journeyman. The pressure developed by the huge wooden screws was so great that he could almost feel it, looking at them, for the top of each of these machines was braced against the ceiling by slanting beams for extra strength. On wires stretched over the men's heads, freshly printed sheets of paper hung drying like laundry, and one of Peter's first tasks was to pull them down and stack them neatly in piles as quickly as the space on the wires was needed for new pages coming off the two presses.

All over the room, where he banged into them every time he tried to run, stacks of paper stood in cabinets, on tables, on the floor, as well as on wall shelves.

He gazed in wonder at two cabinets full of books for sale, which had come off the ships from England, France, and the Netherlands, for this was a bookstore as well as a printing shop. His pleasure increased as he took a few books from the top shelves and found they had been published by his new master. When Andrew showed him a large closet full of these, Peter's chest rose with pride.

The next minute, however, stepping backward, he stumbled over a pile of bundles of blank paper and fell with a crash through the open archway into the type-setting room. As Andrew crossly picked up a switch to thrash him for his awkwardness, Peter scrambled away helter-skelter and banged his shoulder against a type stand, upsetting a tray. Hundreds of tiny pieces of metal, each shaped into one letter of the alphabet, sprayed down over his head.

For the next three hours he slowly and laboriously learned how these pieces of type were arranged in the little sections of the tray, as he sorted them back into place. Other trays on the shelves below were filled with other kinds of type.

In this room Mr. Bradford worked all day, with the pale, tired William, his younger son, nineteen years old. Sometimes even Mrs. Bradford would soil her hands setting up a page or two, though she usually worked upstairs keeping the account books.

Peter found that legally he was a member of this family. He ate at the long table with them, said his prayers with them, obeyed Mr. and Mrs. Bradford—and was slapped and spanked by them when he disobeyed—as though they were his father and mother. He also grew fond of them and was loved by them. Mrs. Bradford tucked the blankets around him at night, and kissed his cheeks, and made him feel that he belonged in the quiet household.

The chore he most disliked was washing the dishes in the evening in a couple of wooden tubs by the fireplace. One night, as usual, he dawdled over them a long time, squatting on the floor in his blue-and-white striped trousers, his canvas jacket unbuttoned, chatting with Mrs. Bradford. She sat rather stiffly, sewing by the light

of a candle suspended from the back of her chair. With her straight brown hair pulled severely into a knot at the back of her head and her straight, pinched mouth, she seemed older than his own mother, who had always been so jolly.

As he would rather talk than work, he asked, "Has my master always lived in New York?"

"Nay," answered the printer's wife, smoothing out the full skirt of her plain gray dress. "Mr. Bradford was born in England, of humble parents, Church-of-England folk. As a lad he became apprenticed to my father, who was a printer, just as thee is to Mr. Bradford now. My family were Friends, or Quakers as they are called, and Mr. Bradford joined our meeting. When he came of age he asked my hand in marriage, and we set sail across the great ocean to make our way in the world. For eight years he was a printer in Philadelphia, but he—" She paused and cleared her throat, then hurried on, "Well, after a little trouble in that city we moved to New York in 1693. Let me see—that must have been four years before thee was born."

"What sort of trouble?" Peter asked innocently.

She looked up crossly from her sewing. "Has thee not finished those dishes yet? Thee is a natural idler! Thee'll never be a rich man, that's one thing certain."

Although he kept quiet then because he had to, he only put off his questions till later. He knew he must find out what his master's trouble had been. This seemed to be Mr. Bradford's special mystery, and Peter felt sure it was important. Evidently it had to do with printing, and when he became a printer himself he would probably need to know.

By and by he added, "I didn't know my master was a Quaker."

"Nay," she replied with some annoyance. "In New York he has been pleased to attend Trinity Church, which is Church of England. However," she concluded with satisfaction, "these past seven years he has been a vestryman—one of their governing board—and that is a position of honor. Will thee *never* finish those supper dishes?"

On Sunday afternoon he rushed off, like a young horse let out to pasture, to a carpentry shop where his brother John was apprenticed. They ran through the muddy streets to a fashionable home on Broad Street, tapped politely at the back door, and were greeted by their mother and little sister. Their mother had become a bondservant nurse to a large, wealthy family. Most of her work was sewing. She made the children's dresses and shirts. Young Cathie must very soon learn to help.

Together the Zengers walked across the Common and into the woods, where John played at being an Indian, climbing trees and shouting war cries. Peter cut down several small trees to build a lean-to, but he spent so much time joking and making the rest of the family laugh that he ended by thinking up a funny song, and the lean-to never was finished.

Every master was required by law to teach his apprentices to read and write and do arithmetic. Sometimes Mr. Bradford himself taught Peter. When he was too busy, he sent Peter to school. But not in the daytime, for Mr. Bradford, complaining of how much Peter was costing him for food and clothes, scolded and shouted whenever Peter was idle for five minutes, as it might mean a pennyworth of work lost. So Peter could go only in the evenings.

Andrew Clarke's Grammar Free-School was one room in the teacher's own house. Peter sat beside his brother John in the smoky candle-lit space crowded with boys and men of all ages bent sleepily over their books. He tried to study very hard, for he wanted to please his master and grow up to be an important printer, too. But he did like to sing and make jokes.

However, as soon as he succeeded in understanding the printed words in English, his fun began. The reader was full of little verses about dogs, cats, donkeys, and monkeys, and he thought them very funny. He began to write humorous poems of his own, which always made his brother laugh and often got him thrashed by the teacher.

But school ended after three months. On his first

24

evening at home again, Mr. Bradford handed him two books to study. Peter read the titles, *A New Primmer or Methodical Direction to Attain the True Spelling, Reading and Writing of English* and *The Secretary's Guide,* both printed by Mr. Bradford.

Peter drew his chair up to the candle that hung near the fireplace and looked at a few pages. "Why, these are books on *spelling!*" he exclaimed, disappointed. He realized suddenly that the life of a printer's apprentice was going to be mostly work and study, with little time for play.

Mr. Bradford bent over him, scowling. "Look at these." He showed Peter a handful of business letters which he had received that day. "See how people spell now! One man writes *hat.* Another spells it *hatt.* One writes *first,* another *ffirst.* Here we see *trial, tryal,* and *tryale, file* and *fyle, morsel* and *morcell.* My boy, we printers are trying to bring order out of the chaos of English spelling. Thee must study hard and learn to spell and print correctly, so that thy readers will learn. This is a great thing we can do."

Peter sighed. Spelling! When he became a printer, couldn't he find something more important than that to do for the world?

CHAPTER FIVE

The Bold Partner

PETER ZENGER had arrived in New York in 1710, and he was an apprentice for eight years. When he became twenty-one he went off to Maryland to open a shop and earn his living.

Almost three years later he was back again, a widower, his small savings gone. He knocked at Mr. Bradford's door, humbly asking for a job.

Although Mr. Bradford wrung his hands and complained that he did not see how he could pay the wages of another journeyman, the truth was he needed Zenger and at last hired him.

After three months Peter married Anna Catherine Maulin, a poor Dutch girl. Almost before he had got used to being back in the city, he was living in a tiny house with her and her two cheerful sisters and her mother. Every evening the little garden was full of neighbors. He was in debt for the first year's rent, but he was happy.

One cold afternoon a disturbing visitor came to the printing shop. His name was Benjamin Franklin.

Although he was only seventeen and poorly dressed, with a loaf of bread sticking out of his pocket, he said he knew all about printing and was already the author of a book. Rather eagerly he asked Mr. Bradford for a job.

His older brother, the young man said, had been publishing a newspaper in Boston, but was in jail for having printed some criticisms of the legislative assembly; so Benjamin had thought it wise to travel.

At this news Mr. Bradford suddenly sat down and stared as though he had seen a ghost.

"I wish to express my thanks, sir," Franklin offered, "for the strong support we received in your son's newspaper in Philadelphia. He wrote that the Massachusetts authorities are bigots, hypocrites, and tyrants, and he—"

Mr. Bradford interrupted. "Well, as you see, I have a journeyman here already." He nodded toward Zenger. "But you might do better in Philadelphia, as my son Andrew there, whose foolhardiness you seem to admire, has recently lost his principal helper by death."

At this refusal Franklin departed sadly into the cold afternoon.

The next Sunday Zenger and his wife attended the old Dutch Reformed Church as usual. As he was too restless merely to sit still, he willingly consented to become the organ blower. His job was to pump the bellows that gave air to the instrument while the organist sat in front playing on the keys, and for this he was to be paid twelve pounds a year.

As they walked to church each Sunday, he felt very proud of his wife, Catherine Zenger. Her straight golden hair was cut short, so that only a little showed under her white lace Dutch cap. In a brick-red dress with a tight bodice hugging her sturdy body, and a big bell-shaped skirt, she strode along beside him, her psalm book dangling by a chain from her arm.

She loved her church and often told her fellow worshipers, "It is a great pity to see the children fidgeting or asleep during the long sermons and learning nothing of religion. We ought to have special classes for them and teach them the stories in the Bible."

Gradually the idea took hold, and a few parents agreed to let her teach their children on Sunday afternoons at the church. She persuaded two or three other mothers to help her. And so was founded the first Sunday School. Later it was copied by other churches all over the world.

Catherine's handsome sister, Ursula Maulin, was soon married to Nick Sijn, a wheelwright. He had one

of the big dusty sheds in which were built and repaired the two-wheeled carts that carried merchandise, freight, or garbage through the streets. A city law limited the number of carts to one hundred and made the drivers walk, not ride. The city's traffic was dangerous enough without galloping carts.

Zenger never spent a penny of money. He put his entire wages into his wife's energetic, pink hands, and she managed so well that he soon discovered he had some savings. It was fortunate that he did, for they soon had two sons. The first they named John, the second, Pieter.

Everyone in the church was soon talking about a quarrel in the Dutch church at Raritan, New Jersey. The people in Raritan were annoyed at their minister. Four men stood up in a parish meeting and accused him of preaching false doctrines.

So he excommunicated the four men. They were forbidden to worship God in any Dutch church. To very religious people, that was a terrible blow. The scandal was discussed all over New Jersey and New York, but most people did not know what the quarrel really was about.

One evening when Peter returned home from work his wife handed him a thick manuscript in the Dutch language. "Look at this," she told him eagerly. "They asked me to read it and let them know if you could get Mr. Bradford to print it."

Peter sat reading the manuscript that evening. Written by the four excommunicated parishioners, it explained what they believed, why they had publicly accused their minister, and why they thought they were right.

Peter became excited over it. "Our people will be glad to see this," he said, "so they can decide for themselves who is more truly religious, these four parishioners or the New Jersey minister."

Next day when Peter showed it to Mr. Bradford, the old printer shook his head. "My son, I have often printed arguments of preachers against one another. But this is different. Good heavens! These four parishioners are attacking their minister who has been set in authority over them! I'd rather not get mixed up in such a scandal."

"What harm can it do?" Peter insisted.

"I've had experience, and I know." Mr. Bradford nodded a warning. "A printer had better not attack the authorities."

"Was that the sort of trouble you got into in Philadelphia before I was born?"

Mr. Bradford looked up sharply. "Never mind that," he muttered, and turned away.

Peter wanted more than ever to know about that old trouble. He could see it had been something important, probably something he ought to know about, to avoid similar trouble himself.

That evening Peter found his wife's sister and brother-in-law and several neighbors waiting uneasily for him in his garden, with four strangers. Catherine came running out of the house at the sound of his voice, and introduced them to him. They were the four men who had written the book.

They looked like sober, sensible tradesmen and farmers, but their faces were drawn and creased with worry. He could see at a glance that being excommunicated was very hard on them.

Peter was embarrassed at having to tell them of Mr. Bradford's refusal. They sighed and shook their heads with despair.

But Catherine clenched her little fists and set her jaw. "Peter Zenger! You go right back tomorrow and tell old Bradford he *must* print that book! I still don't know which side is preaching true doctrine, the minister or these four parishioners, but how can people discuss the question intelligently if the book is not printed?"

Peter admired her energy and courage, which lighted up her pretty face with a deeper beauty than he had seen before. "But Mr. Bradford doesn't want to annoy the authorities," he explained.

One of the four excommunicated men, a thin elderly Dutchman with the saddest eyes Peter had ever seen, told her, "We do not wish you and Mr. Zenger to get into trouble for our sake." He looked sorrowfully at Peter. "But our only hope is for our book to be published."

She thought a minute, then turned to her husband. "We have some money saved up. Ask Mr. Bradford to let you buy enough paper and publish the book yourself, using his press and his type."

When Zenger repeated this bold plan next morning, Mr. Bradford narrowed his eyes. Peter had never seen him look so much like an old fox. "Does thee mean thee would like to be my partner?"

Peter hesitated. "Well—just how would it work out?"

"Thee will buy the paper and do the work," Mr. Bradford answered. "Thee will use my presses, my type, my ink, and so on. And we'll share the profits."

Peter hesitated again. Suppose there were no profits? This was his first business risk. It was also his first fight for a free press with which people could publish their ideas, even against the authorities. Slowly he made up his mind. "Well, I'm not scared."

Mr. Bradford put out his hand, and they shook on it.

Next morning Catherine and Peter emptied their savings out of their little box. Their faces were very sober that day.

For a couple of months Peter was busy, but Mr. Bradford did not complain at his having no time for anything else. The old printer must have known what he was about. He could see that the fight was stirring up plenty of interest. Many people would buy the book, and now if people complained about it, he could lay the blame on his partner.

When the book was published, all the copies were soon sold.

The New Jersey minister rode all the way to New York, crossing the river by ferry in a rainstorm, to knock loudly on Zenger's door and shout angrily at him for half an hour.

"You have poked your compositor's stick into a hornet's nest! Now, three-quarters of my parishioners are reading your book and are sending copies to the authorities in the Netherlands. A meeting has been called. Come yourself Saturday night if you want to see a mob in action!"

But Peter never attended the meeting. Before it could begin, the minister gave in, reinstated the four men, and delivered a long sermon next Sunday to the effect that all Christians should love one another and never quarrel.

Peter proudly fingered his own copy of the book, called *Klagte*. At the bottom of the title page was printed,

Te Nieu-York, Gedrukt by William Bradford
en J. Peter Zenger, 1725.

This was more fun than merely teaching people how to spell.

CHAPTER SIX

Dangers in Printing a Newspaper

BY CHANCE two boys were brought at almost the same time to Mr. Bradford to be apprenticed, but there was so little work he could not take them.

He fidgeted and fretted around the shop all day. Once he said, "I hate to let those two boys go. They look like good workers, and their fathers will pay the fees. But there's not enough business here."

Peter shrugged. "Why don't you start a newspaper like your son's in Philadelphia?"

Mr. Bradford looked at him quickly. "That idea has been on my mind a long time."

Peter said all he could to encourage the timid old publisher.

Next day Mr. Bradford marched off to the grim gray-walled fort to request an audience with Governor Burnet. Because, as the Printer to the King, he received a salary of fifty pounds a year from the government, he felt that he ought to tell Governor Burnet about his plan.

Within a week the shop was buzzing. Every customer wanted to talk about the new paper. Mr. Bradford's first move was to accept the two apprentices.

One of the most eager friends who rushed in to talk was Lewis Morris, Junior, son of the chief justice of the Supreme Court. On a cold, stormy morning in October this young gentleman stamped into the shop, shaking the rain off his greatcoat. He was twenty-seven and a member of his Majesty's Council, which met at the fort with the governor every week or two to pass laws and discuss the difficult business of governing the colony. His thin, pale face was glowing with intelligence and enthusiasm.

"Mr. Bradford," he began eagerly, "I hear you think of publishing a newspaper. A good idea! It's disgraceful for a city of six thousand souls to have no paper!"

"I'm glad you approve, sir," Mr. Bradford answered, smiling.

The young politician jerked two pieces of paper from his pocket and waved them in his long, porcelain-like hand as he added enthusiastically, "I hope you intend making your newspaper interesting, sir. If not, I see no point in publishing it at all."

The printer puffed out his mouth in surprise, trying to hide his annoyance.

"You would do well to begin your very first number with something to set people talking. Here is a little essay I have written." He handed it to Mr. Bradford. "Yesterday I read it in his Majesty's Council. Mr. Alexander was for it, Judge Harison against, and you should have seen them glower at each other across the table!"

Peter said boldly, "May I ask what it is about, sir?"

"It's a firm demand for a tax on all goods brought into New York in foreign ships. That will put a stop to the Bermuda ships' getting all our trade away from us! Mark my words," cried young Morris, his excitable voice jerking upward as he warmed to his subject, "if this action is not taken by our government, New York will be starving within ten years!"

He was just rising on his toes and waving his right arm to emphasize his next statement, when his eye was caught by the opening of the door. He stopped short.

Peter and Mr. Bradford also turned to look.

A neat gentleman carrying a gold-headed cane had entered. He was the only man in New York who wore lace cuffs on his shirt. His cold brown eyes looked from an unsmiling face, as he gave the shop a quick inspection.

"I must be going," young Morris concluded abruptly. "If you want to make your paper a success," he added, shaking Mr. Bradford's hand, "take my advice." Waving to Peter, he barked out stiffly at the newcomer, "Morning, sir!" and departed.

Peter went back to his work at the press, having no desire to speak to Judge Francis Harison, the gentleman with the lace cuffs. Like young Morris, Judge Harison was one of the twelve members of his Majesty's Council. He also held various other offices. He had been sheriff. He had been chief customs inspector, and was now judge of the Court of Admiralty, in which job he had already hanged several smugglers. At the age of forty he was also the recorder (meaning chief judge of the city's criminal courts). He was not rich. The fees he received were small. But nearly all the money he did get he seemed to spend on his clothes.

His words rattled off briskly. "It is rumored that you are about to print a newspaper containing material displeasing to his Excellency the governor."

Mr. Bradford blinked in surprise. Then he glanced at young Morris's article, which he still held in his hand. He folded it quickly and stuffed it in his pocket. "Rumor must travel very fast in this city," he replied, "for it seems to have told *you* what I intend printing before I have found out myself!"

Judge Harison's eyes narrowed with anger, but his

lips smiled more than ever. "I should be only too glad to help you. Perhaps if you would let me see that bit of writing which you just put in your pocket—?" With a sudden flip of his arm, he held out his hand for it.

Mr. Bradford hesitated, and the neat gentleman continued, showing his anger more openly. "You and your partner have already published one book in Dutch that was displeasing to the authorities. You don't wish to lose your title of Printer to the King and the salary that goes with it, I presume?"

Mr. Bradford, his face white with fury, silently took out the paper and handed it over.

The judge put his gold-headed cane under his arm and smiled with satisfaction at this surrender. He held the paper carelessly between the fingertips of one hand, glanced at it a moment, and tossed it down on one of the cabinets full of books.

"Just as I thought," he commented. "This is an outrageous attack upon the policies of our royal governor! If you print it, you will do so at your peril!"

Without another word, he stalked out of the shop.

When he was gone Mr. Bradford said firmly to Peter, "That scoundrel is trying to frighten me out of publishing a newspaper at all! Very well, I accept the challenge. The first number will appear next Monday!"

"Good!" Peter cheered. "And we'll print Morris's article on the front page!"

"And go to jail? Nay, Peter, I am sixty-three years of age and know how to live comfortably in this world."

"But, Mr. Bradford! Maybe Morris is right that in ten years New York will be starving! By what sort of justice can one member of the Council censor an article written by another member of the Council?"

Mr. Bradford shook his head. "Let them settle that between them, and when they are agreed, I'll print what they agree on. My paper will contain no criticisms of the governor."

Peter felt dazed, as though he had been hit by a sandbag. Very sadly he turned back to his work at the press. He could see already that Mr. Bradford's newspaper was going to be uninteresting, and not at all like Andrew Bradford's lively paper in Philadelphia.

"I suppose you've had experience," Peter conceded. Old Mr. Bradford nodded emphatically.

"You don't want to get into trouble again," Peter hinted, "the way you did in Philadelphia long ago."

Mr. Bradford's shrewd eyes looked up sharply. He seemed to be wondering how much Peter knew. Although Peter waited for him to speak, the older man said nothing.

Too bad, Peter thought. This time he felt very close to having uncovered his master's secret.

Then an idea came to him. He picked up the hand-written essay from the cabinet. "May I take this home and read it, sir?"

"Aye, and burn it, too, if thee likes," Mr. Bradford shrugged.

CHAPTER SEVEN

A Newspaper Is Born

MONDAY morning, November 1, 1725, a crowd gathered in Hanover Square in front of the Sign of the Bible to greet the city's first newspaper.

When Mr. Bradford opened the door and held up a handful of copies of the *New York Gazette,* some of the men cried *"Hurrah!"* and two or three boys threw their caps in the air. The crowd pressed forward.

Half an hour later the two young apprentices ran out through the streets, which were ankle deep in gay-colored autumn leaves. The boys shouted happily, waving the papers, hurrying to the homes of all subscribers who had not yet received them.

The only person in the shop who did not share this joy was Peter Zenger. While he was printing the papers, he felt that he was wasting his time. He was tired of working for timid Mr. Bradford. "If I ever have a shop of my own," he thought, "I'll print what I please! The people of New York will have as good a chance as those in Philadelphia to read the truth, instead of this useless drivel!"

He and the other journeyman had never worked so hard at the press. By ten o'clock they had printed more copies than could be sold. Mr. Bradford said, "Peter, slip off thy apron, there's a good fellow, and run with some of these *Gazettes* to the shops and lawyers' offices. Here's a list of important men who have not subscribed. We'll give each a sample copy. See that no one is overlooked."

Zenger strode out into the clear, crisp November day, and it was a relief to feel the sea breeze on his face.

His round of deliveries brought him to Mrs. Alexander's warehouse beside her beautiful home on Broad Street. The leading business people in New York were its fifteen merchants, seven of whom were women. The shop in the front room of her warehouse smelled strongly of fresh, new cloth as Peter handed her a *Gazette* across the counter.

"Oh, thank you!" she said, smiling. "Stay a minute, and warm yourself by the fire. I know my husband will want to see this. James!" she called.

The tall, sloppy-looking man who came shuffling into the shop had such a friendly expression on his homely face that Peter liked him immediately. "Ah, the new

44

paper!" Mr. Alexander exclaimed. "Like a new baby, I'll warrant—*without teeth!*"

Peter smiled sadly at this joke. "Aye, sir, it's guaranteed not to bite."

James Alexander's untidy appearance belied his abilities. He was New York's outstanding lawyer. Also, he was one of the twelve members of his Majesty's Council.

The street door banged open and Lewis Morris, Junior, strode in. "Look at this disgraceful piece of rubbish!" he shouted, waving disgustedly a copy of the *Gazette.*

Zenger never would have guessed that these two gentlemen were close friends and often dined together. Young Morris, whom he had seen at the printing shop, was not more than half Mr. Alexander's size. And the young politician's thin, pale face looked serious and intense, while Mr. Alexander looked as though he was always laughing and relaxed.

"Oh, Peter Zenger!" Morris exclaimed, noticing him over by the fire. "Pardon me for saying that in your presence."

"Not at all, sir," Peter assured him. "I feel heartsick about it."

As he looked from one of these men to the other, an idea occurred to him. Here were two wealthy and influential people who evidently agreed with him about

45

something that meant a great deal to him. Maybe they would help him. Pulling the rumpled little manuscript out of his pocket, he hinted, "I would gladly print this article of yours as a pamphlet, if I had a shop of my own."

The look they both shot at him told him they understood. For a full minute no one said anything. They seemed to be considering his suggestion. He waited. What would their verdict be?

The three men were nearly the same age, but were very different in appearance. Zenger wore a workman's clothes and his own sand-colored hair; the two gentlemen wore brown silk suits and short-tailed, horsehair wigs.

They stood looking at their copies of the *New York Gazette*. It consisted of a sheet folded once, making four pages 7½ by 12 inches with two columns of print on a page. It contained gossip from England—the doings of the King and the noblemen—also war news from Europe, and a list of the ships that had entered or departed from New York harbor recently. Nothing else.

"Zenger," Morris snapped, "if you want a shop of your own, why don't you start one?"

Peter's breath suddenly returned. His neck felt hot and his hands wet. "My wife and I have figured it out. It would take ninety-three pounds to buy a press and

type and printer's tools from London." He shrugged
and tried not to show how hopeful he felt.

"Well, you have savings, haven't you?" Morris demanded.

"We could pay half of it," Peter admitted.

"Oh, Mr. Alexander and I will lend you the rest."
Morris turned to go, as though the matter were settled.
Fifty pounds was the price of a couple of horses, no
very serious amount to him.

Mr. Alexander, who was a Scot, laughed heartily.
"You're always so quick to spend my money!"

Morris waved his friend aside and said to Zenger, "I'll
talk Alexander into it, and my father, too. Order your
printing machine. New York is strangled and gagged
without a free press. No one will say I'm not good for
fifty pounds for a worthy cause." Suddenly he turned
and came back again. "By the bye, give me that article
of mine. I've discussed it with another member of the
Council, and he wants to write it over again—longer
and sharper! We'll give you something to print that will
make people talk about the Zenger press!"

CHAPTER EIGHT

A Shop of His Own

EARLY in February Peter looked around Mr. Bradford's shop for the last time. He was worried about his new venture. He and his family would starve if his business was not a success.

Mrs. Bradford tottered in to say good-bye. Though no older than her husband, she was already feeble and in bad health. Peter put his arm around the little old lady tenderly. She had been like a mother to him.

Mr. Bradford's parting words were, "I expect we'll be coming to visit thee in jail soon, if thee keeps on with those wild ideas of thine. I tell thee, if thee prints every quarrelsome political essay that comes into thy shop, thee'll stir up the crowds of bondservants, apprentices, and poor laborers to riot and burn down the homes of their masters. Go easy, my son!"

The tiny shop that Zenger had rented was up on

Smith Street near the City Hall. (The name has now been changed to William Street, and the exact spot is in the block between Maiden Lane and Pearl Street.)

The next day Zenger, with the help of his brother John, the carpenter, was setting up his new press. Young Morris rushed in, waving the much expanded article in his slim, white hand. "I'm sorry you'll have to print it without any name!" he complained. "My friend received most of this information from our enemies and hopes to get more; so we must not tell that he wrote it."

When Zenger set the essay in type it was thirty-six pages. It roused all New York. Hundreds of men came eagerly to his new shop to buy copies. But no crowds burned down any buildings.

For a while the Zengers did well. Catherine's friends in the church brought four books in Dutch to be printed, and also a book of sermons by a Dutch minister, translated into English (called *The Adorable Ways of God*).

They had more work than Peter could do alone, so Catherine came to his rescue. In the time she could spare from housekeeping she sewed the pages together and began to study the mysteries of bookbinding. Peter was amazed to see how quickly she could learn. Before the year was out, she could set type and do everything in the shop except operate the press.

His brother John also was rising in the world. He

spent his small savings for tools and rent and opened a little furniture-making shop of his own. Peter Zenger ordered two new chairs and a larger dinner table to accommodate his growing family.

His mother had died many years before, but his sister Cathie was twenty-one and that year at last had consented to marry Peter's stolid friend Fred Bekker. Fred and Cathie opened a small tavern, where the poorer folk of the neighborhood could come in the evening to talk politics over a mug of ale.

But trouble began for Peter. Most people did not bring their business to the new printer. He worked slowly, made mistakes in spelling, and his bindings were not very neat. Only the Morris family remained loyal to him. Chief Justice Lewis Morris of the Supreme Court sent a slave with an interesting official pamphlet for him to print. It was a legal opinion on witchcraft, saying there were no witches in New York.

Everyone was glad to find this out, and Zenger sold many copies.

But for several years he had less than one book a year to print. Only small odds and ends were brought to him —a deed to some land, a contract or two. With his family growing larger, he had less and less money coming in.

But the church at last consented to pay him the small salary it had promised him for pumping the organ. His friend Hendrick Michael Cook became the organist and began to give Peter lessons on the big, noisy instrument. Peter loved it. He looked forward to becoming an organist himself.

In September, 1729, a piece of news in the Philadelphia *American Weekly Mercury* brought him to his feet with a start. Clapping his hat on his head, he marched off hurriedly to call on his former master, Mr. Bradford.

The old printer's son, Andrew Bradford, was in jail. He had been publishing a series called the "Busy-Body Papers" written by Benjamin Franklin and his friends. One of these articles was in favor of liberty and against hereditary power. It had been written by a friend of Zenger's, the Reverend Dr. Campbell of Long Island, and had so alarmed the authorities that they had arrested Andrew Bradford and locked him up.

Zenger tapped at the Sign of the Bible on Hanover Square and began to say to old Mr. Bradford, "I'm so sorry about your son—"

But Mr. Bradford interrupted him. "Come in, Peter. It's not so bad as all that. Andrew is smart. Here's a letter I received half an hour ago. He has talked the authorities into letting him go." Though it was a cool day, Mr. Bradford sat down and fanned himself. "But it was a narrow escape. Let that be a warning to thee!"

Zenger walked home again very soberly, not knowing just how to take this. If he himself were arrested, would he, too, be able to talk his way out? Or would he be tried and punished?

One idle afternoon only a month later, when he was glancing sleepily through a newspaper, the Pennsylvania *Gazette,* he noticed that it had been bought by a new publisher, Benjamin Franklin. The first page said, "There are many who have long desired to see a good newspaper in Pennsylvania . . ."

Zenger was surprised. Stretching himself as though he had just waked up, he called to his wife, "Catherine, come listen to this!"

She clattered down the rickety wooden stairs, and he read it to her. She laughed. "If people in Pennsylvania desire to see a paper better than Andrew Bradford's *American Mercury,*" she said, "imagine how people here in New York must want a better newspaper than his father's timid, stupid *New York Gazette!*"

"If I had enough money, I would print one!" Zenger exclaimed.

Catherine took Franklin's paper and sat down on the bottom step with her chin on her little fist. She began to read it.

"I don't understand that man," Peter confessed. "Franklin is running a printing shop in Philadelphia as a rival to young Bradford, and I'm running a printing shop in New York as a rival to old Bradford. The only difference is that Franklin is making a success of it, and I'm not!" He sighed. "Franklin's about ten years younger than I am, too."

"Don't give up hope," she answered, turning the page. "Some day you and I will publish a newspaper like this! Just as lively, too. This man Franklin certainly knows what kind of news is interesting. Look." She brought the paper to her husband. "He starts right off with stinging comments on the political fight up in Boston. Let's sell his paper here in our shop, and study it ourselves every week! We can learn how he does it!"

CHAPTER NINE

The New Governor's First Words

IN THE year 1731, Zenger's friend Hendrick Michael Cook, who had been teaching him to play the organ, moved over to the new Dutch church, which had just been built, and Zenger was appointed organist in the old church. He loved the powerful instrument and enjoyed pressing his strong, blunt fingers on the noisy keys.

The governor of New York died suddenly, and months passed before the King of England bothered to appoint another. Meanwhile Rip Van Dam, oldest member of his Majesty's Council, had to be acting governor. This was a tiresome job, but it paid him a good salary.

Peter was conscious of these changing political events,

but he did not think they concerned him directly, although he liked the old Dutchman. Zenger had printed business papers for Van Dam, had often visited his shipyard west of lower Broadway, and had recently played a lullaby on the organ just for fun at the baptism of Van Dam's first great-grandchild.

The evening of July 31, 1732, Zenger ran eagerly down to the waterfront, for he had heard that the new royal governor was arriving at last. Stars, the innumerable glittering, soft stars of summer, glowed all over the night sky. A welcome cool breeze from across the wide harbor made the lamps flicker in the hands of servants and slaves.

Zenger got there early enough to secure a place at the front of the crowd near where the old shipbuilder was standing with the other officials. They all peered at the lights and flapping sails of a great warship that moved slowly up to the stone wharf.

"I don't know why I feel nervous," he heard old Rip Van Dam confess. The president of his Majesty's Council was seventy-two, a little bowed with age, but still as round as a barrel. His thirteen months as acting governor were at an end tonight. New Yorkers had been amazed at his rule, for, unlike most governors, he had not taken the opportunity to make himself rich at the expense of the taxpayers.

The welcoming committee of councilmen and leading merchants remained huddled together anxiously watching the big wooden ship as the sailors and long-shoremen tied her to the wharf and ran out the gang-plank.

First to come ashore were a dozen soldiers, who ranged themselves in two lines at the end of the gang-plank, raised their long guns with bayonets in place, and stood awkwardly at attention.

Marching between them came a short, stout man in a bright red military uniform that seemed too small for him. He strode quickly down onto the wharf, sticking his chin out importantly. Zenger easily guessed that this was the new royal governor, Colonel William Cosby.

He was followed by Lady Cosby, their sons Billy and Henry (large, frowning young men), and their two daughters, pretty young ladies aged sixteen and eight-een. The women seemed to drift across the wharf as though on wheels, for their great billowing skirts con-cealed their feet.

Lady Cosby looked homely and ill-tempered, though Zenger had heard she was a sister of the powerful Earl of Halifax. In front of her ran a yapping little dog, which she held by a silk ribbon.

Mr. Alexander, having been a member of his Maj-esty's Council longer than most of those present, stepped forward. "Your Excellency," he began formally,

"this committee wishes to extend its welcome in the name of the—"

Cosby shouted in his face, "Don't speak to me until you're spoken to!"

The tall lawyer glowered with annoyance, but did not retreat.

The new governor put his fists on his hips, stuck his elbows out, and faced old Rip Van Dam. "You must be the Council president they've told me about!" he growled.

Van Dam gave a ceremonious bow. "We are greatly honored by your Excellency's arrival among us."

"Yes, yes. Very good." Cosby sounded more friendly now. "You've been acting governor since the death of what's-his-name, I presume."

"To the best of my ability, your Excellency, and aided by the peaceful, loyal temper of the populace."

Cosby became even more friendly. "I suppose you and the legislature have provided my salary for that time."

Zenger was astonished. He saw old Rip Van Dam gasp and heard a ripple of protest among the other officials standing near by. The old Dutchman answered in amazement, "Your Excellency's salary begins today!"

"Rubbish!" the new governor roared, his face turning red in the lamp light. "Don't talk nonsense to me!"

His anger only made Van Dam stubborn. "Your Ex-

58

cellency can scarcely expect a salary for the time before you began to work!"

"Began to work?" Cosby bellowed, doubling his fists and strutting up and down. "Began to work? What do you think I've been doing? Working for this province by lobbying against the Sugar Bill in Parliament, as you well know! Thunder and brimstone! I'll have you understand I intend to be rewarded for my services!" He stamped his foot and waved his hairy fists for emphasis. "Show me this miserable shack you call a governor's mansion!" he snorted, and marched away.

CHAPTER TEN

The Fighters Assemble

SO MANY friends and relatives came to Zenger's shop to buy newspapers and to gossip, that he heard many rumors. Most of the poorer people were becoming alarmed at the new governor's behavior.

When a farmer's cart stood in his way on the road, Cosby ordered his coachman to beat the poor farmer with a horsewhip. Though the man was nearly killed, there was no way he could even protest afterward. A poor farmer could not cause the governor to be arrested and tried. As Mr. Bradford's newspaper did not mention the incident, few people ever heard of it.

Governor Cosby stole a deed to some Indians' land and burned it. And when he granted new lands to men who applied in the legal way, he made them give one-third to him; so he soon secretly acquired huge estates. None of these things was even mentioned in Mr. Bradford's *Gazette*.

Old Rip Van Dam cried out with amazement when he received a demand for nine hundred pounds, half the salary he had received as acting governor. That was enough to buy a large house. Stubbornly he refused to pay.

The governor knew that no jury in New York was likely to believe that Van Dam owed him that money; so Cosby ordered a new court to be formed, which would try the Dutchman without using any jury.

In one of old Rip Van Dam's warehouses, a new theater was opened. Peter and Catherine, in the cheapest seats, sat waiting expectantly. Like most New Yorkers, they had never seen a play, had never been inside a theater. At first they believed everyone in the city was there, it was so crowded. But then Peter noticed that no seat had been prepared for the governor. A number of officials who were wealthy and prominent in society had absented themselves from the opening of New York's first theater. Zenger began to wonder why. Had they taken sides against good old Van Dam? How could they?

Evidently Governor Cosby had friends. Peter was alarmed when he realized that their anger had become so aroused that it had made them miss even an occasion like this. There was going to be trouble in the city, serious trouble.

At last he began to see how these events would concern him. In a political fight, a printer would be needed.

When the curtain rose, he and Catherine felt very strange watching men and women walking about and talking on the stage. The play was a comedy from England called *The Recruiting Officer*. Most of the first act was over before they could get used to it. But some of the scenes were so funny, they began to laugh.

During the intermission about half the audience stood up and walked about, laughing and greeting their friends. Zenger noticed the lawyer Mr. Alexander, his head above the crowd, whispering to one man after another. Zenger wondered. Looking around, he saw Van Dam doing the same.

As he strolled through the crowd with his wife, Peter was greeted by Van Dam. His round old face was creased with anxiety. "Have you heard the news?" the elderly shipbuilder asked in Dutch.

Peter nodded. The customers in his shop had argued all day about Governor Cosby's new court with no jury.

"And what do you think of it?" Van Dam persisted.

Peter answered softly, for many of the people crowding around them might understand Dutch. "Why won't he let a jury decide? His new court to force you to pay him is plain tyranny!"

The old man gripped his hand. "We are counting those on our side. We shall have to stick together!" He hurried on to speak quietly to someone else before the curtain went up for the next act.

CHAPTER ELEVEN

A Brave Printer Was Needed

THIS new court, which seemed so dangerous, was to consist of the same judges who sat in the Supreme Court. But Chief Justice Morris (the father of Mr. Alexander's friend) had not been consulted about it.

As soon as Governor Cosby tried to use the new court, by suing Van Dam in it, Chief Justice Morris furiously denounced it. From his judge's bench he astonished the courtroom by arguing that for the governor and Council to set it up against the will of the people's elected assembly was outrageous. "And therefore," he concluded loudly, "by the grace of God, I, as chief justice of this province, shall not pay any obedience to them in that point!"

He stood up abruptly and walked out of the courtroom.

Next Monday morning Peter and Catherine Zenger

eagerly read Mr. Bradford's *New York Gazette*. As they expected, it did not mention that the chief justice had defied the governor's tyranny.

Catherine threw down the useless paper and went back to sewing a coat for her little daughter. "Now that the chief justice has joined the others against the new governor, things are going to begin to happen. Surely they'll want the people to learn what the governor is up to. Haven't they asked you to publish a newspaper for them?"

"We might suggest it," Peter said hopefully. He tied on his big leather apron and seized the handle of his press with a grin. "Now at last maybe we'll have our chance!"

Late that evening Mr. Alexander, seeing the light on, came stumbling into the shop and asked to see the printed copy of the judge's speech, which Zenger was preparing as a pamphlet.

Lewis Morris, Junior, hurried anxiously in after him. He had just left the City Hall, where he had been working with a committee of the provincial assembly, which had already voted against the new court.

Morris, then thirty-four (a year younger than Zenger), had a brilliant mind. He lived with his beautiful wife and six-year-old son in Westchester County, where he ruled as owner, lawmaker, and judge of his father's vast estate. He was no longer a member of his Majesty's

65

Council, having been expelled for his vigorous, biting remarks. But he had quickly been elected to the legislative assembly instead.

As Zenger stood up politely to welcome these gentlemen and dust off two chairs for them, he wondered if they, too, felt the need for a paper and had come to sound him out about it.

Swift and sharp as usual, Morris asked his friend impatiently, "Can you let me see those letters that came for you on the ship today?"

At the sound of the men's voices, Catherine, who had been sewing in the children's room above, ran down the rickety stairs.

"I have a reply from my friend in London," Mr. Alexander said, taking a letter from his pocket. He shook his head, evidently worried. "This Cosby is the tenth son of an Irish nobleman."

"*Tenth* son!" Zenger exclaimed. "That must mean he's poor."

Mr. Alexander continued, "A short while ago he was governor of another colony—the little island of Minorca in the Mediterranean."

Catherine asked, "Was he a better governor there than he seems to be here?"

"He was good to himself," Mr. Alexander answered glumly. "He stirred up a quarrel with a Spanish merchant who owned a shipload of snuff valued at 9,000

66

pounds in money. Cosby seized the snuff, sold it, and began spending the money on clothes, wine, and a new carriage. But the people of Minorca sent a complaint to London. The officials in London found Cosby guilty of illegal acts and called him home!"

Young Morris burst out, "This is the man they have sent us for governor! Why?"

Catherine gave her opinion. "I can guess the answer to that, sir. He must have powerful friends."

"Aye, the Duke of Newcastle," Mr. Alexander read from his letter, "and the Duke of Grafton. And we knew that Cosby is brother-in-law to the Earl of Halifax." Halifax was the King's secretary of state for colonies.

Morris commented, "Then we shall find him hard to get rid of. He'll be more cautious this time, and with friends like that—!"

Zenger asked, "I've been wondering what sort of man he is personally. Is he clever?"

"Listen to this." Mr. Alexander read from the letter in his hand, while Zenger held a candle for him. " 'Colonel Cosby has had but little schooling, is unintelligent, has no common sense, and believes that might makes right. His one idea is to get money, and his only notion of diplomacy is to use force. His disposition is haughty and pompous, and he has a violent temper, over which he exercises little or no control.' "

Young Morris struck the counter with his fist. "The King's agent in New York, with full power over us and over our property!"

Mr. Alexander turned to the printer. "How do you like the latest news? Governor Cosby has expelled the chief justice."

Zenger confessed honestly, "I'm not sure I understand it."

"It means," the lawyer explained, "that from now on, whenever the governor happens to dislike you or me or anyone, he can order us to be arrested on some false charge, and when we try to defend ourselves, he'll say to his judge, 'Find that man guilty, or lose your job!'"

Zenger saw his wife making signals to him over her sewing. Now that the time had come for him to speak up, he felt that publishing a newspaper would be dangerous and also a lot of work. At the last minute he almost remained silent. But he met Catherine's steady blue eyes, and before he knew what he was doing he opened his mouth and suggested, "It's too bad New York has no newspaper that will warn the people."

Young Morris was pacing restlessly about the shop. Suddenly he stopped. "I suppose you've heard that we're forming a new political party in order to fight this governor and try to have him sent home or at least make him behave himself. We're the Popular Party, and we'll defend the rights of the people. Mr. Alexander has been chosen to lead us."

"Congratulations!" cried Mrs. Zenger. "You can count on our support."

Mr. Alexander raised his shoulders, set his homely jaw with determination, and thanked her solemnly. Then he added, "We shall need your support, for our party must have a newspaper."

Morris asked definitely, "When are you going to print a newspaper for us? We need one to defend the people against this government!"

Mr. Alexander nodded approval.

Zenger suddenly felt as though his big hands were in the way. "I've been saving a little money for one," he hinted.

Morris shrugged. "Oh, that! If Mr. Alexander will be the editor, you can count on me for the finances. I'll go around with a hat. Mr. Van Dam will put in ten pounds. So will my father. Every leader of the Popular Party will contribute."

Zenger made one more request. "To print a newspaper every week, I'll need a journeyman."

Mr. Alexander thought a moment. "I'll write to my friend Mr. Andrew Hamilton in Philadelphia. He has mentioned a young printer who is a great friend of his, Benjamin Franklin. Probably between them they can find us a printer's helper."

69

Zenger knew that printing a newspaper could get him into serious trouble. He had seen Mr. Bradford being warned by Judge Harison.

Zenger felt uneasy. What would he print first? And what would the governor do to him? Especially now that Governor Cosby could give orders to the judges—

CHAPTER TWELVE

The Westchester Election

MR. ALEXANDER hurried into Zenger's shop to report that one of the assemblymen from Westchester County had died, and that Governor Cosby would have to order a special election to replace him.

Mr. Alexander's friendly face was wrinkled with excitement as he explained, "It's our first chance to test the strength of the new Popular Party! We'll give our answer to Cosby for expelling Judge Morris from the Supreme Court! We've persuaded Judge Morris to stand for election in Westchester. All those who support Governor Cosby will vote for his candidate, a schoolteacher named Forster. All those who don't want the governor to have the judges under his thumb will vote for Mr. Morris!"

"I'll print this handbill for Mr. Morris immediately," Zenger decided, looking at the papers the lawyer had given him.

"And now is the time to launch our newspaper!" Mr. Alexander added. "I'll get you a journeyman from Philadelphia before this week is out. Mr. Bradford will print nothing about this election in his mealy-mouthed *Gazette,* and the people of New York must hear of it and must understand exactly what it means!"

Just as the sun was rising Monday morning, October 29, 1733, ex-Judge Morris and his supporters entered grandly upon the village green at Eastchester town (now called Mount Vernon). With a shout of triumph the fifty men who had been on guard there since midnight, to prevent any tricks by Governor Cosby, scrambled onto their horses and joined the parade. To the amazement of the townsfolk who stood watching, over three hundred horsemen, with their horns blowing, paraded three times around the green. It was a larger number than had ever appeared for the election of one man since the settlement of that county.

Three taverns ringed the green, facing St. Paul's Church. Two of them, Joseph Fowler's and Mr. Child's, were well prepared. Mr. Morris had sent wine, food, and his own servants from his huge estate of Morrisania near by to help cook it. Some of his neighbors had done the same. With appetites sharpened by watching and riding in the frosty autumn night, the voters made a merry feast.

About eleven o'clock in the morning loud catcalls from the green drew all the men out to see what was coming. Zenger, leaning from a window of one of the taverns with a thick slice of bread in his hand and a thick slice of ham on it, saw Governor Cosby's candidate, William Forster, come riding up the country lane from the east at the head of a troupe of horsemen.

William Forster, the governor's candidate, had been a poor teacher in a school run by a church in Westchester. But somehow he had managed to pay Governor Cosby a hundred *pistoles* to appoint him clerk of court in that county. Now he wanted to be elected to the assembly, too. (A "pistol" was a Spanish coin, much used in New York, worth about four dollars.)

Zenger almost dropped his ham in his excitement. Reminding himself that he was here to report this for his newspaper and must get all the details, he pulled his head in again and ran out the door. This first experience as a reporter made him feel important and also a little bewildered. How much would he dare to print? What if he printed something the governor disliked?

He watched the parade around the green. Following the governor's chosen candidate, two gentlemen rode carrying flags. After them, Zenger was amazed to see, rode James Delancey, the new chief justice of the Supreme Court, and Frederick Philipse, the other judge. Zenger heard one of the men of the Popular Party ask, "What's Judge Delancey doing here? He doesn't live in Westchester."

"Neither does Mr. Alexander," another answered. "He's here as leader of our party, and Judge Delancey's here as leader of the Court Party. Sort of to give 'em courage. But their side needs it more. Look how few they are!"

Zenger counted 170 horsemen, about half as many as were for ex-Judge Morris. Zenger laughed.

Mr. Morris stood in the front row of the watchers. Forster passed with a stony face. Judge Delancey and Judge Philipse, who came next, had sat in court with Mr. Morris for two years. As they rode by, Philipse very civilly saluted Mr. Morris by taking off his hat. Morris gave a little start of surprise, smiled briefly, and doffed his hat in return.

But Zenger's laugh died and his breath almost stopped as he saw Judge Delancey set his jaw, stare straight ahead, and ride by without a gesture. That face, with the white marks of anger streaking down across the cheeks, clearly showed that this was no polite difference of opinion between gentlemen. This was a fight.

The Court Party rode only twice around the green. Being outnumbered almost two to one, they were glum.

They retired to the third tavern, where Judge Delancey (who was very wealthy) had paid in advance for a dozen roast legs of lamb.

Zenger was interested to see that a number of sober-looking Quakers had joined Mr. Morris's side. He could tell them because the Quakers wore no silver buckles in their hats, no silver buttons on their coats, nor any other decoration.

An hour after Forster's arrival, another shout went up. "Here comes the sheriff!"

His name, Nicholas Cooper, was printed on the notice of this election, but Zenger had never seen him before. He was a grim-faced man, so short that he was almost a dwarf. The horse he rode was such a beauty that the men whistled. One cried out, "I know who that saddle belongs to!"

Everyone crowded forward to look. The sheriff had a war saddle, pistols, and sword, all decorated in scarlet and the weapons richly chased with silver. Somebody shouted, "That pistol belonged to Governor William Cosby a week ago!"

"So did the sword!" cried another.

"And the horse, too!" Zenger yelled. His son John had made him take an interest in Cosby's horses.

All the voters on both sides poured out onto the green. The sheriff stood on the little rise of ground in front of the church, unrolled a paper, and read aloud very fast. It was not important whether anybody understood the words. These men had been to county elections before and knew that the sheriff always began by reading the governor's writ, which gave him power to count the voters. At the end of it, he bawled out, "I bid the electors proceed to the choice!"

Judge Delancey and Candidate Forster interpreted this as meaning that the count would be taken the easiest way, by simply lining up the two sides opposite each other. "All loyal voters for the governor's choice stand to the right!" the young chief justice commanded.

Mr. Morris, the ex-chief justice, gladly accepted this challenge and called his friends to gather behind him. They were feeling happy-go-lucky, laughing and cheering, because they were obviously more than the governor's party.

But the sheriff (appointed by the governor) scowled at the result. He muttered and waved his short arms. "A poll has been demanded!" he bawled, meaning that each voter would have to be counted separately.

"Who demanded it?" Mr. Alexander asked loudly, stepping forward and looking extra tall in his huge, rumpled overcoat. No one had heard anyone demand a count. "How can you say someone has demanded it, when no one has?"

"A poll must be had," the sheriff answered stubbornly.

77

Mr. Morris stepped up and asked firmly, "Which side shows a majority?"

"A poll must be had," the sheriff answered again.

Mr. Morris repeated his question twice, becoming angry. But the sheriff continued to give the same answer. The lord of Morrisania, who had been instantly obeyed all his life, could scarcely contain his fury.

The sheriff led the way to a tavern, selecting the only one that had a front porch. But both sides argued and wrangled so much that two hours passed before tables, chairs, and benches were set in place, two clerks appointed and two inspectors for each party. At last the voting began.

Each man stood up in front of the whole crowd, gave his name, and told which candidate he voted for, for the secret ballot was unknown. However, that old system had one advantage. Neither the sheriff nor Governor Cosby could fake the counting of the votes, all of which were cast in the presence of nearly five hundred witnesses. Zenger kept count, Mr. Alexander kept count. So did many others.

When one man was offering to vote for Morris, a Court Party inspector challenged him, insisting he owned no land or house or cattle or other property worth at least forty pounds in Westchester County. Therefore he was not entitled to vote.

Several of the man's friends called out that they knew him and he was entitled to vote. But the sheriff, not satisfied, insisted, "Bring a Bible, and let him swear to it!"

There was a delay while someone ran to the church across the green and returned with the sacred book. The voter laid his hand on it, swore that he was a free-holder, and voted.

Soon a man with no silver buckle in his hat came to the table and gave his name. "I vote for Mr. Morris," he announced firmly.

The other candidate, Forster, whispered to his two inspectors, who promptly demanded, "Does he own enough property?"

Several of Morris's men called out that they knew the Quaker well and would witness to the fact that he owned an ample estate.

The sheriff, becoming very much excited, demanded order, and held out the Bible to the Quaker. "Will you solemnly swear on this book that you own an estate?"

The Quaker stepped back, and immediately there arose a storm of protest from the Popular Party. Everybody knew that Quakers were forbidden by their religion to swear to any oath and that the law gave them the special right of giving their "affirmation," which meant more to them than an oath to most people.

The Quaker said in the same firm tone as before, "I give thee my solemn affirmation that I own an estate in Westchester worth many times forty pounds!"

The sheriff, however, insisted, "If you won't swear to it, you can't vote."

At this there was a furious outcry from Morris's friends. Mr. Morris himself told the sheriff, "How dare you say such a thing? This form of voting by Quakers has been accepted at every election, for it is specifically allowed in the laws of England and in the laws of the Province of New York! And, having been chief justice of the Supreme Court for eighteen years, I should know!"

The lawyers, Mr. Alexander and his partner Mr. Smith, each told the sheriff the same thing. As the crowd knew that these two had read more law books than anyone else in the whole colony, they pressed round eagerly to listen. Mr. Smith squared his broad shoulders and bellowed, "To refuse the vote to a Quaker on such grounds is against the law and is an unpardonable violation of human rights!"

But the sheriff had suddenly become deaf.

One of the Popular Party supporters asked, "Who is this sheriff, anyway?"

Another said, "I never saw him before!" Everyone began to discuss him.

Zenger soon learned that the new sheriff was a stranger, who had never lived in Westchester County. According to law and custom no man could be sheriff unless he owned an estate in the county and had lived there for some time.

Mr. Alexander slapped his big three-cornered hat on the back of his head and exclaimed, "I can see that Governor Cosby has appointed him on purpose to run this election his way!"

Delancey, the new chief justice of the Supreme Court, stood silent through all this. He also was supposed to know the laws, but he said nothing. Judge Philipse, who himself had been elected to this same legislative assembly a few years before, must have been familiar with the election customs. But he wandered about, looking confused, keeping his mouth shut.

In spite of all the outcry the sheriff refused the vote of every Quaker, one by one. Thirty-eight of them would have voted for Mr. Morris.

The mood of the Popular Party had now changed completely. They were angry, sullen, noisy.

The voting was delayed by so many arguments that it lasted nine hours. The bonfire was built up again, lanterns were lighted, the stars came out.

At eleven P.M. the count stood: 231 for Morris, 151 for Forster.

Everyone was tired out. Even the sheriff looked haggard. But he still asked, "Is there anyone else to vote?"

Complete silence.

Making a sour face, he turned to Mr. Morris and announced, "You are elected. I wish you joy!"

A cheer rose from the Popular Party.

Zenger smiled grimly, knowing what a scandal this election would cause when he printed the story. And perhaps the governor would be angry.

CHAPTER THIRTEEN

A Test of Power in the City

WHEN Peter returned home next day he heard the sound of booming cannon in the celebration at the fort for the King's birthday. But it was not the King's birthday that excited him. While his wife and children eagerly listened, he paced about the shop, telling what he had seen, and acting out the election. Catherine and his son John (then ten years old) asked many questions.

But when Zenger sat at the counter in his shop to write the story, he did not know how to begin. After a minute he offered the quill pen to his wife.

As she took her place before the blank sheets of paper, she announced, "We are going to let the people of New York know about the cheating the governor's sheriff did, no matter if we risk our lives!"

With a firm look on her pretty face she wrote all

83

afternoon and again all evening, taking time off now and then to feed the youngest baby, Evert, who was only a year old.

Next morning she read her article to her husband. He was surprised by the simple, clear way in which it was written. Then together they crossed out every personal opinion of their own, leaving only the facts.

Mr. Alexander hurried into the shop with a package in his hand. His big, long face looked more cheerful than ever. Behind him came a sturdy-looking stranger, evidently a working man, for he wore his own hair (as Zenger did) instead of a wig. "I've got you a journeyman printer at last," the tall lawyer cried happily. "Just in the nick of time! Can you print the first number of our paper by Monday?"

Zenger answered boldly, "We can if we have enough articles to put into it."

Mr. Alexander opened his package on the counter. It was full of papers. As he was the leader of the Popular Party, his friends had agreed he should edit the party's newspaper. Zenger was pleased and proud to be working with such an important person.

"We'll begin with this." Mr. Alexander unfolded a hand-written sheet. "It's a short sermon on wisdom by a preacher friend of mine."

"Good!" Mrs. Zenger commented. "It will be like announcing in a loud voice that the first thing needed in New York newspapers—something that has been conspicuously lacking—is wisdom!"

Mr. Alexander nodded, smiling. Beside it on the counter he laid a poem, "To show that our paper is going to be entertaining and will not put people to sleep. And here," he added, "are some London newspapers and several letters from friends of mine in England, telling of events in Europe. Somebody will have to select what's most interesting and rewrite some parts to make them fit in the space we have."

"My wife can do that," Zenger volunteered.

The editor looked doubtful, but said, "I'll be much obliged to you if you will try, Mrs. Zenger. I'll talk with you about it and point out which items seem to me most important. Perhaps my wife can help you when she's not too busy running her store."

Catherine timidly showed him the long article she had written about the Westchester election.

"Oh ho!" he exclaimed. "This is what I was going to talk about next. Let me read it!" He sat down to it and asked for a pen.

Zenger showed the new journeyman around the shop. They examined the press, and the man talked as though he understood how to print.

Mr. Alexander looked at his watch. "I have to hurry," he announced, scrambling to his feet. "This is a good article, Mrs. Zenger. I've changed very little of it. I

85

think I can trust you with the foreign news, after all. Now, what sort of heading can you put at the top of our front page?"

"We want to copy Mr. Franklin's paper," Catherine answered promptly, reaching down a pile of old copies. Each was labeled: *"The Pennsylvania Gazette, Containing the freshest Advices Foreign and Domestic."*

"Since Mr. Bradford has already used the name *Gazette*," she went on, "we thought our paper could be the *New York Journal, Containing the freshest Advices Foreign and Domestic."*

Zenger added, "Because it's going to be a sort of journal or diary of life in this city."

The lawyer looked thoughtful. "That's good," he mused, "but, strictly speaking, *journal* is a French word meaning 'daily.' We can't print this more than once a week."

Zenger gave a wry smile. "Then let's call our paper *The Weekly Journal."*

They copied Benjamin Franklin's heading, his plan of arranging the articles on the pages, his note about the subscription price at the end of the last page, and even the kind of type he used.

About five o'clock cannon began to boom again. Peter's son John dashed out into the street. A moment later he reported, "Everybody's running toward Broadway! Something important must be happening!"

The crash and rumble of cannon continued. The Zenger family hurried out to investigate, and soon found themselves in the midst of a crowd.

The merchant ships anchored in the bay right under Governor Cosby's nose were firing their guns to welcome ex-Judge Morris and celebrate the Westchester election!

A crowd led by some of the outstanding merchants gathered at the wharf to greet him as he stepped ashore from a sailboat. The Popular Party formed a parade to boast of their victory. When Zenger saw what was up, he left his family among the watching, cheering crowd and marched with his friends.

Ex-Judge Morris walked ahead, a little man but startlingly handsome, well-known in this city. His son, Lewis Morris, Junior, walked with the gentlemen behind him. Now father and son both were members of the assembly and would fight shoulder to shoulder. The noise had brought huge crowds, and when they recognized the leader, cheers broke out gaily all along the way.

Mr. Morris was escorted to the Black Horse Tavern, where a handsome dinner was prepared for him at the expense of the gentlemen who received him. The banquet room was decorated by a tablet hung in the middle of one wall, which said in large letters: "KING GEORGE—LIBERTY AND LAW!"

87

CHAPTER FOURTEEN

Zenger's Newspaper

O N MONDAY morning the first customers gathered at dawn in front of Zenger's shop shouting for their copies of the *New York Weekly Journal,* for the rumor was that the paper would contain whatever news Mr. Bradford was afraid of. By nine o'clock the first edition was sold out. Soon a crowd of a hundred men milled about in the street waiting for more.

Rushing the frames of type back into the press, Zenger and the journeyman took turns printing as fast as they could. John, ten years old, and Pieter, who was eight, helped by keeping the inkpads filled, folding and drying the printed sheets, and running to fetch more paper.

Catherine had her hands full writing down the names of subscribers, as each laid three shillings on the counter for the first quarter of a year.

When the second edition began to come off the press, the crowd outside surged forward. Some men stood reading their copies aloud to those near by. Others quickly folded theirs into their pockets and hurried away. Catherine guessed that the latter were supporters of the Court Party, and wanted to read the paper in private.

As more and more copies went out the door, the noise and amazement in the street increased. Nobody paid any attention to the few errors. Zenger had been so excited, he had printed the date "October 5, 1733" when it was November 5, 1733. He had printed *agoin* (for *against*), and *Teusday,* and *geting,* and *presisted.* But when Catherine finally noticed them, she thought, "Considering what a rush we were in, we did pretty well."

Men ran through the streets with the paper in their hands to show it to their friends. Like Bradford's *Gazette,* it was only one sheet folded, printed on both sides, making four pages, each 7½ by 12 inches.

Catherine's article told the whole story of the Westchester election, stressing how the sheriff had violated the Quakers' right to vote.

Before the day was over Zenger had begun to print a third edition.

Late that night, after the journeyman had gone home and the family had climbed upstairs to bed, he stood sleepily with the last candle in his hand taking a look around the shop with weary satisfaction. He had given New York something to think about. More money had come in than on any previous day of his life. But also he was in danger.

Someone rapped on the door. He turned and looked at it with suspicion. New York was such a quiet town that scarcely anyone ever was out on the streets at this hour, after ten o'clock.

The knock sounded again. Peter set down his candle, picked up a heavy composing stick for a weapon, and unbarred the door with his left hand.

It opened immediately, and Mr. Bradford, now seventy years old but healthy as ever, stepped quickly into the shop. He held a copy of the new *Weekly Journal* in his hand. "I have come to tell thee the history of my youth, my son," he began, coming right to the point as usual. "It has long been a secret, but I tell it to thee as a warning."

He pointed to the paper. "Here in print thee has accused our royal governor of accepting a bribe of one hundred *pistoles*. Thee has pinned an election fraud on a sheriff, who can be appointed or dismissed only by the governor and is therefore a representative of the governor. Listen to me."

The Printer to the King sat on a tall stool beside the

counter. "When I was under thirty—some five years before thee was born—I was a friend of George Keith in Philadelphia. He was a Quaker leader, like William Penn. But Keith and I wanted to change the Quaker religion. We were tired of sects and wanted all Christian churches to join together. Is there anything wrong in that? I still think it the best plan. We printed pamphlets attacking William Penn, attacking Governor Fletcher, attacking everyone who disagreed with us. I was young then and full of enthusiasm. Well, to make a long story short, I was arrested. My type, paper, and other printer's equipment were seized by the sheriff. At length I was tried by a judge and jury. I had no lawyer to defend me; I spoke up in court, cross-examined the witnesses, and defended myself."

Zenger asked anxiously, "What did the jury decide?"

"They were out discussing their verdict for two whole days. In the end they reported that they could not agree. So the judge had to let me go. Governor Fletcher of Pennsylvania sent for me and gave me some sober, fatherly advice. When I promised him I would behave myself better in future, he got rid of me by a curious device. He arranged to have me appointed Printer to the King—*in New York!*"

"But if the jury had found you guilty—?" Peter mused.

Mr. Bradford answered softly, "They would have cut off my ears, and the hangman would have whipped me through the streets with a horsewhip." Rising and going to the door, he concluded, "I tell thee this for a warning. Good night."

CHAPTER FIFTEEN

Three Drunken Sailors

THE first response was disappointing.

Governor Cosby appointed Judge Francis Hari-son to edit Mr. Bradford's paper so that it could answer the *Journal*. Zenger watched Judge Harison going by on the street. He swung his gold-headed cane and tossed his long lace cuffs, trying to make up for the fact that he was small and rather effeminate. People said that he was a good dancer and that he often tagged around after Lady Cosby.

Mr. Bradford must have been annoyed at having this fancy gentleman come and edit his *New York Gazette*, for Harison had once tried to frighten him out of publishing it at all. However, as Printer to the King, old Bradford received fifty pounds a year from the government. Consequently he did as he was told, for he loved money. Although he had not been consulted, he accepted the new editor.

Zenger eagerly read the next number of the *Gazette* to see what threats it would make against him.

He found that Judge Harison had written several columns describing Cosby as a good and noble governor. But not a word about Zenger.

Zenger felt uneasy, as he crumpled the *Gazette* between his big, bony hands. What did its silence mean?

Each week the *Journal* lashed out vigorously. Not naming any particular governor, it said, "Some governors may certainly err, misbehave, and become criminal." It said that Governor Cosby had destroyed the deed to the Indians' land, and that Cosby had illegally dismissed the chief justice of the Supreme Court for refusing to take orders.

As Zenger could not be solemn all the time, he wrote jokes for his own paper. A laughing paragraph described "a large spaniel about five foot five inches high," whose initials were "F.H." Anyone could guess that it meant Judge Francis Harison.

All over New York people sat wide-eyed with astonishment, reading the pages, which seemed to sizzle in their hands. Never before had they seen such energetic writing. Zenger himself did not always know who wrote the articles, for Mr. Alexander gathered them and brought them in unsigned. When he took a trip around the city, Zenger found that in all the taverns men were talking about the *Journal*. Some cheered and laughed. Others were angry and growled that the printer ought to be hanged.

In the mansion inside the heavy stone walls of the fort Governor Cosby stared at the *Journal*. He was so poorly educated that he scarcely knew how to read. Struggling through a page or two of the new paper, he could not make out all the words, but he could see that someone was attacking him. Who was it? Who was running this nasty paper? The only name on it was that of the poor printer, who obviously could not do it alone.

Cosby immediately thought of the old shipbuilder, Rip Van Dam, who still refused to pay him nine hundred pounds, half the salary Van Dam had received as acting governor. Probably he was financing this paper.

Cosby threw the newspaper on the floor, stamped on it, and swore that he would ruin Van Dam and thereby stop the paper.

He thought of a way. He had already summoned Mijnheer Van Dam to court so many times that the old Dutchman had at last become bored and was simply staying home and not coming into the courtroom any more.

Governor Cosby believed that the next move would be easy. He called Attorney General Bradley to help.

They would claim that Van Dam could not be found,

that he was a fugitive from justice. If this claim could be presented in court when he was not there, they would be able to seize his entire estate, including several ships, some valuable houses, the shipbuilding yard, and the new theater. But first they must persuade three witnesses to sign the claim.

Governor Cosby himself found a way to accomplish that.

On the night of January 10, 1734, a dirty, ragged bum entered a water-front tavern and spoke to Mrs. Hawkins, the landlady. He had a fawning manner and smiled too much, so that his thin, red mouth looked like a gash in his bristly cheeks. "I want to see my mates as lives here, Billy Spinks and Billy Fearn. Kindly be so good as to tell 'em their friend Marsh is here, formerly their shipmate on Governor Cosby's ship, the *Seaforth*."

When Spinks and Fearn came downstairs, they welcomed their old pal.

Spinks was a wiry little Englishman, equally keen for a nose-breaking scrap or a friendly bout of singing. He would often become the best of pals with a man he had knocked down, if he thought his opponent had put up a good fight.

He slapped Marsh's back and offered him a drink.

"No, no!" Marsh insisted. "Tonight the drinks are on me!"

Spinks only laughed. He knew that ever since Marsh

had been mustered out of the crew for stealing some of the ship's tar and selling it, Marsh had been out of a job.

Fearn seemed amused, too, though he was trying to look sympathetic. He was fat and good natured even when sober, and ten times more friendly when drunk.

The two sailors felt superior, standing beside the ragged bum. Their long hair was tied in back and was stiff with black tar. They kept their hands in the pockets of their tight, belled white canvas trousers and shrugged their shoulders under their blue slip-over canvas jackets.

"You don't believe me?" the ragged fellow protested. Reaching in his pocket, he pulled out a handful of coins, which he held glittering under a lamp. But where he had got them he would not say.

Several hours later the three sailors were so drunk they could scarcely sing any more. Spinks noticed that Marsh seemed less drunk than he and Fearn, but Spinks himself was too far gone to care.

Marsh at last began to come to the point. "I've a paper about the old Dutchman—you know—what's his name?—Van Dam, the one they say's out on's head."

"Out o' whose head?" asked Fearn.

"The Dutchman," Marsh repeated. "He can't talk straight."

Spink wagged a warning finger at him. "Thash what happens if you drink too much whisky!"

"I been trusted with a paper about him," Marsh

continued. "And I know you old pals of mine'll do me the kindness to sign it for me."

Fearn shook his head. "Shine nothin'. They hang you!"

"No!" Marsh protested. "There's naught o' harm in it!" He swore many oaths that what he was telling them was true.

Although Spinks wanted to be friendly, he did not like this idea. He got one eye focused on Marsh and objected, "We don't sign nothing without our captain's orders. Long live Captain Long!" He drank.

"Long live Captain Long of the *Seaforth!*" echoed Fearns. "And I'll knock any man's eye out as says different!"

Marsh assured them, "The captain knows all about this paper! If you'll sign, he'll be as much obliged to you as the governor will!"

"Thash different," Spinks admitted. "Let's shee the paper."

Marsh took out a parchment and laid it folded on the table. Spinks noticed uneasily that Marsh kept his dirty hand on it.

"Whashit say?" Spinks asked, hiccoughing.

"Oh, 'tis all legal nonsense," Marsh assured them. "Don't mean nothing." He moved his hand a little and read a few words, " '. . . the person herein named is not to be found.' " Marsh explained, " 'Tis only to sign

your names here after me. Let me sign first. So help me, you won't never be called to no account for it!" Swearing many oaths that this was all true, he called to the landlady for pen and ink.

He signed his name under the words on the parchment, and Spinks and Fearn, half dead with the whisky and wanting to help their old friend, signed after him.

Late the following afternoon, in a shed on their wharf, Spinks and Fearn sat on a couple of tar barrels and watched the snow slowly drifting down over the harbor.

"I don't like it," Spinks asserted. He had a headache and felt very sober. "Who gave him that money, and what for?"

"Ask me," Fearn agreed; "that paper's poison."

"What was in it?" Spinks asked, and after a moment added, "We jolly well better fish after it. We may be in trouble."

They did not know where to find Marsh, but one of the soldiers on guard at the fort was a friend of theirs. They shuffled through the snow to see him and asked questions. But he did not know anything.

"If you get a chance," Spinks concluded, "ask the clerk."

Fearn added, "You'll maybe save us from a heap of trouble."

Returning by way of the fashionable residential block of lower Broadway, they passed their captain's house. They stopped to speak to the handsomely dressed Negro slave who was shoveling snow away from the door.

"Hey, Caesar," Spinks asked, "is it true what Marsh told us, that the captain knows about that legal paper?"

"Ain't seen Marsh in a long while," the big slave answered. "What paper do you all mean?" When they described it, he promised, "I think I can find out."

Two days later the soldier came to see Spinks in Mrs. Hawkins' tavern. "The clerk says yon paper was an order to arrest Mr. Van Dam, the president of his Majesty's Council."

Spinks swore violently. "Now we're in for it! Why didn't that skunk Marsh tell us?" He called Fearn, and they consumed several beers as they grumbled and worried over this news.

"If we land an important man like that in jail," Spinks fretted, "and the captain don't happen to like it, he'll string us up by our thumbs. 'Tis our own stupid fault!"

While they were still undecided what to do, the tall slave, Caesar, marched in, dressed in Captain Long's handsome green-and-gold livery.

Laughing, he told them, "You all in a peck of trouble! Captain want to see you right now, quick. Come on!"

"What's so funny?" Spinks demanded.

"You'll see." The slave swiftly led the way.

Shuffling through the snow again, the two sailors humbly entered the fine house where their captain stayed.

This was Captain Robert Long, who had given a banquet to Governor Cosby on board the battleship *Seaforth* the day of the Westchester election. He was a public-spirited man (later he built a wharf for the city at his own expense) who had always been loyal to Cosby as long as he thought Cosby was a gentleman.

"What've you two been charting with that scoundrel Marsh?" he demanded as soon as he saw the sailors. "Understand this: I'll have none of my crew battened to a crooked eel like him! Now, spit it!"

When they began their story of Marsh, the unexplained pocketful of silver, the whisky, and the parchment, Captain Long's face darkened. He was the commander of a battleship, and when he grew angry, he made other men tremble. "I never heard of it!" he snapped, squaring his powerful shoulders.

When they finished, he began giving orders. "You're a pair of fools!" he roared. "Only a couple of blockheads would sign such a thing! March right up this street, you tar-headed idiots, to the notary's office. Tell him I sent you! Squirt the whole filthy story in his ear, and make him write it down! Then you sign it, and tell the notary I said he's to deliver a copy to Mr. Van Dam!"

The sailors stood fumbling with their hats. "Aye, aye, sir!" they answered, and hurried away, glad to have got off without even a beating with the cat o' nine tails.

CHAPTER SIXTEEN

The Grand Jury

OLD Van Dam's hands were trembling and his mild eyes looked rather bewildered, but his round chin was set as stubbornly as ever when he stumped into Zenger's printing shop with the two affidavits, one signed by William Spinks and the notary, the other by William Fearn and the notary.

Catherine gasped as she read these papers. But her husband was not at home. "He has stepped over to the City Hall. They say something's going to happen in the Supreme Court today."

Zenger found a crowd already gathered in the courtroom. He felt puzzled because many faces turned to look at him as he entered. Some pointed at him. He heard others ask in whispers, "Who's that?" and their neighbors reply behind their hands. Wondering what was the matter, he sat down as quickly as he could.

A grand jury of nineteen New Yorkers, their names drawn by the sheriff from the voter's book, had just assembled. Some were men he knew at least well enough to nod to on the street. It so happened that three rich merchants were included. They sat waiting for either the attorney general or the judge to tell them some evidence against someone. Zenger did not yet know who it would be, but they would be asked to vote for an accusation against somebody. If a majority of the grand jury voted to indict any man, he must be arrested and tried.

Zenger wondered who it would be.

The clerk called all persons present to stand. The two judges entered and took their places, looking solemn, self-important, and a little nervous. There used to be three, but Governor Cosby had arbitrarily reduced the number to two when he dismissed Mr. Morris. Although judges in New York did not wear the special wigs and robes of the English courts, they did manage to make themselves haughty and impressive. Clerks marched in ahead of them, solemnly carrying books. The judges entered one by one, each in a magnificent embroidered silk suit trimmed with solid gold buttons and gold braid.

Judge Delancey, a young man, looking just as pale and intense as he had at the Westchester election, sat in the seat of the chief justice, fumbling his papers, while the clerk asked the nineteen jurors to stand, place their hands on Bibles, and swear to give a true verdict.

Zenger watched the new chief justice carefully. Now that judges could be dismissed at will by the governor, it was obvious that he had to take orders from the governor.

The new chief justice was the leader of the Court Party. Son of the richest merchant in town, Delancey had gone to college at Cambridge University in England. His tutor there, who had become his loyal friend, was now Archbishop of Canterbury, powerful in the British government. Young Delancey was clever. He had found his classes so easy that he had not worked hard, had never liked to study. He had raced through a year of law school in London and had been easily admitted to the bar.

On his return to New York his cleverness and money continued to help him to get ahead. He married the daughter of a wealthy old politician and built himself a magnificent mansion on Broadway near Trinity Church.

When the jurors sat down, he began immediately to read to them in an eager, irritated tone, barking out his words. "You must have observed that recently there have been several papers printed with a design and a tendency to alienate the affections of his Majesty's subjects of this province from the governor whom his Majesty has thought fit to set over them!"

Zenger sat up suddenly, with a feeling of shock, as though he had been hit on the head with a stick. He was the only printer whose papers had attacked the governor.

"And in particular," the judge rushed on, "some men with the utmost virulency have endeavored to bespatter his Excellency with foul reports and injurious charges. They have spread abroad many seditious libels, in order to lessen in the people's minds the regard that is due to a person in his high station."

At the words "seditious libels" Peter Zenger's face began to feel cold and then hot. If anything printed in his newspaper were proved to be a libel, he could have his ears cut off. And if it were proved to be seditious, he would be hanged.

"The authors are not certainly known," the judge admitted, "and yet it is an easy matter to guess who they are that, by making use of Mr. Van Dam's name, have gained some credit among the common people."

Judge Delancey talked to the jury for half an hour, hoarse with anger, saying that liberty of the press was dangerous. At last he concluded, "I know most of you personally" (an odd thing for a judge to say, for it sounded like a threat) "and I make no doubt that you will discharge your duty." He indicated that they were to indict either Mr. Van Dam or Zenger.

The jurors marched off to the jury room and stayed all day.

The long wait was hard on Zenger. At first he smiled and shrugged, but as the hours dragged on, he felt more and more depressed and weary.

When the court adjourned for the night, he hurried home. Catherine tried to cheer him. And he did perk up over the news that Van Dam had learned of Cosby's attempted trick with the three drunken sailors.

"Half the town's going to start yelling when we publish these two sailors' affidavits!" Zenger agreed heartily. But he added, "If I don't get locked up before I can print them."

Next morning he returned uneasily to hear whether he was to be arrested and tried. He felt danger creeping close to him.

The foreman bowed to young Judge Delancey and began reading from a paper in his hand. "If it please your Honor, the Grand Jury of the County of New York make their humble address to this Court, that your Honor the chief justice will favor the public in having your Honor's charge to us printed."

He paused.

The judge gave a strange smile and almost shrugged. "The Court will consent to this request," he decided.

There was a silence. Everyone waited for what would come next. Zenger felt as though his heart had stopped beating.

The judge said, "You may continue."

"That's all the jury decided, your Honor," the foreman answered, looking with a worried expression to see how the judge would take this news.

Delancey controlled his temper with difficulty. The jury had disobeyed him. However, in a choked voice he concluded, "The case is closed."

The jurors were dismissed and sent home.

Zenger sat still, half dazed. Suddenly he realized that for the past five minutes he had hardly breathed. He had said he "did not scare easy," but now after the danger was over, he could feel that *something* queer had been going on inside him.

People crowded up to him and began shaking his hand. Some were friends or customers. But he also recognized several of the men who had looked at him so suspiciously when he had entered this courtroom yesterday, now congratulating him and smiling.

One of the jurors, shaking his hand, whispered in his ear, "Some of the jury wanted to indict you, but they couldn't persuade the majority. Go ahead and print!"

CHAPTER SEVENTEEN

Zenger's Press Stops the Governor

A FEW days later John, Pieter, and Mrs. Zenger sat sewing the fresh copies of Mr. Van Dam's sixty-eight page pamphlet. Some parts had been written by his two lawyers, the tall Mr. Alexander and the learned Mr. Smith. The old shipbuilder had written the rest in Dutch, which the Zengers had translated into their blunt, homely English. Their *New York Weekly Journal* was announcing it very plainly:

ADVERTISEMENT

There is now printing and will shortly be published and to be sold by the printer of this paper, *The Proceedings of Rip Van Dam, Esq., in order for obtaining equal justice of his Excellency William Cosby, Esq.,* by which it seemeth that said Van Dam believes an attack has been made in this province on the privilege of juries.

Dozens of customers burst into the shop demanding, "Where's this pamphlet as says the governor won't give good old Van Dam the right of trial by jury?"

Some hurried away with it. Others sat down in the shop to read it, pointing out bits to one another.

Catherine's brother-in-law Nicholas Sijn came early for a copy, read it slowly, and discussed each page with the latest customer.

It told the whole story. "Great suffering walruses!" cried the honest wheelwright. "Cosby's going to arrest him!" he shouted to a fat old woman with two live hens slung over her shoulder, their feet tied together with a string. She had come in to buy a newspaper.

"Nay, there you're wrong!" she replied. "The grand jury refused to indict."

Nick was dancing up and down. "Not Zenger! Van Dam! Cosby knows more tricks than you think! He got three drunken sailors to sign a paper! Oh, walruses! Wait till I tell my neighbors about this!" He fled out of the shop.

The news spread. Crowds gathered at street corners all over the city, holding the pamphlet in their hands and talking in low, angry voices.

"If they can put Van Dam in jail and seize his property on a charge signed by three drunks, what good are the laws? Or is this governor superior to the laws?"

"Let them try to arrest him! That's all I say. Let them try! Blood will flow in the streets of New York! And the first house we'll burn down is Judge Delancey's!"

Mr. Alexander hurried to the printing shop, rubbing his hands with anxiety. Head and shoulders taller than the men by the door, who stood aside to make way for him, the lawyer paused to tell them, "You can see the power of the press with your own eyes today! I've walked all through the town, and the whole place is seething over this scandal of the drunken sailors!"

Inside the shop he found Hendrick Michael Cook, the musician, leaning across the counter, saying to Zenger, "Look you, Peter Inkpad, if his Excellency can do this to an important man like Van Dam, who has two expensive lawyers to defend him, what will Cosby do to you or me if we happen to say anything he doesn't like? Now, I ask you, what will he do to you and me, that cannot pay anyone to defend us?"

The power of the press broke through the grim, gray, twenty-foot walls of the fort.

Governor Cosby sat by one of the fireplaces in his draughty banqueting hall, playing checkers with an officer of the regiment. The Van Dam pamphlet lay on the table beside his wine glass. Two buttons of his red military coat were unbuttoned where it felt tight. His melancholy Irish setter leaned against his knee, having its shiny red head rubbed from time to time. The late January afternoon was so dark with snow clouds that half a dozen candles were burning and fluttering around the governor.

The soldier on guard at the door announced, "The Honorable George Clarke, of his Majesty's Council, to see your Excellency."

"Send him in!" Cosby replied gladly, and looked round from his game. "Sit down, George! Have a glass of old Madeira."

"Thanks, I don't mind if I do." The large, stout, elderly Mr. Clarke lowered himself comfortably into a chair. He owned more land than anyone else in New York. "Ah," he commented, his fat cheeks looking even more solemn than usual, "I see you have the new pamphlet. A bad business, that."

Cosby was surprised. He picked up the booklet and regarded it with dull eyes. "Haven't had time to look through it yet," he offered as an excuse. The real reason why he had done nothing to Zenger yet was that Cosby was not able to read well. Consequently he did not know that every Monday morning the *Journal* was calling him a criminal.

The landowner informed him, "You'll find Mr. Van Dam has printed the whole blessed story of Marsh and the paper signed by the sailors!"

Governor Cosby's face turned suddenly deep red. "How in thunderation did he get hold of that?"

Mr. Clarke was never excited by anything. Calmly he replied, "Every man in New York that can read has got hold of it now." He described the angry groups discussing it all over the city.

Cosby knew that back in 1709 Governor Cornbury had gone to jail. He also knew that the stubborn Dutchman, Van Dam, had been one of the principal leaders of the people against Governor Leisler, who had been publicly hanged in 1691. Cosby trembled with fear. Gripping the arms of his chair, he asked almost in a whisper, "What do you think they'll do?"

"I'm not sure," the wealthy councilman answered, looking him straight in the eye. "But I'd rather not drive them to begin it and then find out."

Cosby leaped up so violently that he knocked his wine glass and bottle onto the floor. Striding up and down, he swore ferociously.

When he paused for breath, Mr. Clarke advised calmly, "Maybe we could forget about this plan to arrest Van Dam."

"But the sheriff already has a warrant to seize him on February seventh!" Cosby stormed.

At this piece of news Mr. Clarke at last showed that he felt disturbed. Opening his eyes wide, he raised his huge body out of the armchair. "I'll drop by and speak to the sheriff this evening. Is there anything you'd like me to tell him?"

"Yes!" roared Cosby, the veins in his neck swelling with anger. "Tell him to tear up that cursed warrant, and if he even remembers I ever gave it to him, I'll skin him alive! Hell and damnation! I have nothing but a measly two hundred soldiers to protect me, but that Dutchman has a printing press!"

CHAPTER EIGHTEEN

The Fighting Press

THE fight was on. Both sides became more violent. Zenger's *Journal* demanded to know why New Yorkers must be governed by "a fellow only one degree better than an idiot." The paper asked if he thought he could govern intelligently by merely swearing, and added, "He has nothing human but the shape."

As Zenger set up these words, picking the metal letters one by one from the type case and arranging them in the iron composing stick in his left hand, "i-d-i-o-t," he thought he could feel them sizzle up his arm. He laughed.

Catherine came and looked over his shoulder to see what was so funny. But she frowned. "Sometimes I wish our writers would not use such strong language." Her voice sounded frightened. "It makes me uneasy."

"Aw, fiddle-faddle!" he shrugged. "Do we have free

speech here, or don't we? Why should we always be polite and conceal our feelings? We're going to let people know that some of us feel plenty strong about that baboon in a red coat who governs us."

Reading the *Gazette,* he at last found replies. Editor Judge Harison now wrote articles that mentioned Zenger and the *Journal* by name. Zenger smiled as he sat on his doorstep in the summer evening, reading old Mr. Bradford's paper. Although this might mean danger, it was more fun than fighting against silence.

But evidently Harison himself felt that his replies were not good enough to have much effect, for he soon tried more direct action.

He wrote an unsigned letter which threatened the whole Alexander family. But Zenger boldly printed the letter word for word, with the sworn testimony of witnesses who recognized the handwriting. Harison had to abandon the rest of the plot to harm the Alexander family.

Zenger patted his ink-spattered old press. "This machine has saved the lives of two very important people. Who'll be next?"

The *Journal* published facts. Zenger pushed hard on the handle of his press, and out came strong, mouth-filling sentences. Governor Cosby's special court, which was to operate without any jury, was illegal. The newspaper firmly stated the reasons why.

As Judge Harison in the *Gazette* was unable to answer, the result was that that special court never did try a single case. The governor seemed afraid to use it as long as Zenger's paper was going.

Zenger cheered. In his garden in the evening his brother-in-law, Nick Sijn, pointed out, "There's no telling how many people you've saved by stopping that court!"

Zenger especially enjoyed setting up the articles about the editor of the rival paper. These paragraphs told in detail how a grand jury had voted to indict Judge Harison for having kept a man nine weeks in jail on a false charge. (The man was a former friend and law partner, with whom Harison had quarreled.) By law, Harison should be tried for this crime.

But Governor Cosby got his hands on the indictment. Defying the law and the grand jury, he tore up the piece of parchment and let Harison continue to edit the *Gazette.*

Zenger himself wrote one of the articles about that:

What good is an indictment? Fiddle-faddle, give the goose more hay! Suppose a man in public office should knock your brains out with a brick. Your widow will tell the grand jury, and he shall be indicted. Pray, what notice will be taken of that? Mayn't the great man do as he pleases?

The *Journal* stated that in Westchester the governor had illegally appointed a stranger to be sheriff, and the

sheriff was arresting innocent people. As Zenger printed this, he remembered the new sheriff at the Westchester election.

The *Journal* listed one dishonest action after another, and openly demanded that Cosby be sent back to England. While he was governor, the writers declared, men's lives and properties were in danger.

Unable to answer these stinging attacks, which were painful because they were true, Judge Harison again resorted to desperate methods.

On Saturday evening Zenger, assisted by his family and his journeyman, worked late to print enough copies of the *Journal* on his one rickety, creaking hand press. His son John stood on a chair to set type. Little Pieter hung the damp sheets like laundry on the wires overhead. Catherine read proof, while rocking the baby to sleep.

Next morning at church, while Zenger was climbing onto the organ bench, a Dutch stevedore whispered to him that last night, while the printing had been going on, Judge Harison and three friends had paraded into a waterfront tavern and ordered the sailors, stevedores, and sailmakers who were drinking there to attack Zenger's shop and burn it down. Harison had talked a lot and offered bribes, but the men had refused to follow his orders.

Drawing in his breath, Zenger boomed an angry series

of loud chords on the organ that made the whole congregation sit up.

The next week he printed the story, which caused
another scandal. Every trap the governor's supporters
laid was snapping back against them for the same
reason: Zenger printed the story.

On the first of May Zenger moved. He had so much
business and such a large family—six children—that
his old shop was no longer big enough.

While he, his brother John, and the journeyman
were heaving the clumsy press into place in the new shop
and spiking the braces from it to the ceiling, Catherine
and her sister Maria carried pots and pans to the kitchen
in the rear. They hauled the bedding upstairs and began to give a homelike look to the small attic rooms in
which the big family were going to live. Pausing a moment in her work, Catherine poked her head out a
window. In front of her was the bridge over the canal,
which ran up the middle of Broad Street.

Across the street she could look into the big handsome
home and gardens of Mr. and Mrs. Alexander. Mrs.
Alexander had even built a sidewalk a full block long
in front of her house, her warehouse and store, her husband's law offices, and her neighbors' houses. When
strangers came to New York, the townspeople showed
them Polly Alexander's sidewalk. Never having seen
one before, they boasted that she had invented it.

As she turned her head, Mrs. Zenger could see almost next door the grand four-story brick mansion with a whale walk on the roof, built by Stephen Delancey, father of the chief justice. (This building was later known as Fraunces Tavern, scene of Washington's farewell to his officers, and is still standing.) Beyond she saw the ships in the harbor. In the opposite direction was the big brick City Hall, built right across the street, looking sleepy and peaceful in the morning sunlight. The whole quiet, luxurious neighborhood seemed an odd contrast to the fury of the battle being waged on that machine downstairs.

CHAPTER NINETEEN

A Hotly Fought Election

THE battle suddenly flared into action in September at the city election. A crisis had arrived.

The city government consisted of mayor, recorder, and sheriff appointed by the governor, and fourteen aldermen (two from each ward) elected by the voters.

In the city a man could vote even if he did not own a house—provided he was a tradesman or master craftsman. For instance, Zenger could vote, and his brother-in-law Fred Bekker, who ran a tavern, could vote, though a man who merely drove a cart could not.

Thirteen of the aldermen, most of whom had been re-elected year after year, were known to be supporters of the governor. There were a good many complaints against them. The rich objected that the aldermen gave themselves all the contracts for buildings and roads. The poor complained that the aldermen forced them to dig down a hill and put a new road through it, all for no wages. And though the city was infested with beggars, the aldermen had done nothing to help them.

Worst of all, the aldermen had not even tried to punish Judge Harison.

But this time the Popular Party challenged them by offering candidates of its own. Zenger printed handbills, which the Popular Party distributed. He himself wrote a funny pamphlet about a group of laborers discussing the aldermen. It set half the city laughing. Encouraged, he wrote a political song and printed it.

On Monday, September 30, two years after the arrival of Governor Cosby, the election astounded everyone who watched it.

As soon as Zenger got his newspaper off the press, he hurried out to vote.

At the polling place he found three Court Party men working for the governor, openly pouring out mugs of beer and whisky. One of them, not recognizing him, offered Zenger a mug of beer, saying, "Vote for our men. You'll never regret it."

Zenger only laughed.

But his neighbor the blacksmith accepted a shot of whisky, saying, "Oh, your candidates are fine fellows, I'm sure!" and then stood up and loudly voted for the Popular Party men.

This caused a great deal of laughter on one side and sincere curses on the other.

Walking to the next ward, Zenger found that the vote had reached 35 for the Popular Party against 5 for the governor's men. Though more citizens stood waiting to vote, Zenger saw the end of it.

One of the losing candidates was a well-dressed lawyer named John Chambers, who had been alderman for several years. Though he was known to be a supporter of the governor, he was no fool. When the vote was going so strongly against him, he shook his rivals' hands, congratulated them, and declared the election finished.

Zenger hurried on down to the South Ward in time to see Judge Harison—lace cuffs, gold-headed cane and all—march up to the polls to announce his vote, followed by a dozen friends. Loud cheers from one side and hisses from the other greeted him as he gave his name. This election was especially important to him, Zenger knew, because half the aldermen would be judges of the city's courts and could try even Judge Harison.

Chief Justice Delancey, white-faced with anger as usual, stalked up to vote, leading fifteen soldiers of Governor Cosby's garrison. Shouts of protest burst from the crowd. Zenger was sure the soldiers had no right to vote.

But Judge Delancey, the leader of the Court Party, insisted that these fifteen had slept in this ward the previous night and could vote. The clerk accepted them.

A well-known merchant appeared and voted for the Court Party candidates, though everybody knew he lived in another ward.

Despite this cheating, the total vote for the two Court Party candidates in the South Ward was only 45, against 49 for the Popular Party men.

All day long the city was full of singing and shouting, with groups of drunken voters staggering home from the polls bawling insults or singing Zenger's song. Dogs barked, two horses ran away, and a startled herd of cows stampeded through the streets. It was a good day for women and children to stay home. None of them did, for they all wanted to watch.

Zenger went home late that evening, tired and excited, wondering how the governor was going to take this defeat. Would he accept it meekly, or was he a fighting man?

CHAPTER TWENTY

The Counterattack Begins

ZENGER'S son John shouted that the new aldermen were marching up the street. The printer tucked up one corner of his leather apron and hurried to the open doorway to wave to them.

The brittle October sun shone on their handsomely wigged heads. Most of them smiled when they saw him, and waved back.

Twelve of them were new. Only one Cosby supporter had been re-elected—by a small margin, 38 to 37. Since the fourteenth, Mr. Styvesand, was not a governor's man, no one had run against him.

As they passed the shop, one of them paused to whisper to Zenger, "The governor has just given us a talking-to. He's thinking of you."

They marched on toward the City Hall.

"Ahem!" said Zenger. Suddenly he felt that the autumn was turning cold. He shut the door.

On Monday the *Gazette* printed what the governor had said to the new aldermen. Zenger read it by the light of the evening fire. It was a strong speech.

"I call your attention to a paper printed in this city touching your elections, in which it is wickedly insinuated that they were 'carried against the governor's interest,'" Cosby began. He then insisted that he had had no interest in the election and demanded that the writers and the printer of that paper be suitably punished.

Zenger thought this sounded serious. Although the governor might not read very well, he evidently had understood the election results.

While Zenger sat worrying over the newspaper, he heard a knock at his door. His wife and her sister looked up from their sewing. He could see fear in their faces.

But when he opened, he found a committee of five aldermen. While the women bustled about, clearing stacks of paper and type off two more chairs, one of the visitors handed Zenger a thick manuscript.

"Here's one of our copies of the new City Charter. Though it's nearly four years old, it has never been printed. Surely the people have a right to know how their city government is supposed to function. What do you think?"

Zenger felt a sudden warm glow inside him. The

governor had ordered them to punish him. Instead, they were bringing him a reward.

Chuckling, he began to discuss the price.

Catherine lighted extra candles and served mugs of beer to the gentlemen. After half an hour's talk Zenger signed an agreement with them. He was to receive seven pounds (a large sum of money to him) and give the city six printed copies of the charter. The rest of the copies that he would print he could sell for three shillings each. It looked to him like good business.

For a month he worked on it whenever he could find spare time from the *Journal*.

His newspaper accepted the challenge in the governor's speech. The false claim that the governor had had no interest in the city election was easily answered. The *Journal* published proof that he had actively helped his candidates.

Governor Cosby found an answer for that.

One afternoon Zenger's sister Cathie burst open the door and rushed in, her eyes wild with terror. Silently she handed him a printed paper. When she could catch her breath she told him excitedly, "Every tavern is required to post copies of it."

Zenger read. It was an order by his Majesty's Council that certain copies of the *New York Weekly Journal* be "burnt by the hands of the common hangman, or whipper, near the pillory in this city on Wednesday, the 6th instant, between the hours of eleven and twelve in the forenoon."

He felt puzzled. What did the Council expect to accomplish by that?

"There, there, Sister," he consoled her. "I suppose they're trying to warn me. But don't fret yourself."

He gave her back the handbill. "Here, nail this on the door of your tavern, where everyone can see it. We'll soon find out whether we have any friends."

Next morning Mr. Alexander stumbled hurriedly into the shop. "How's your courage, Zenger?"

The printer grinned. "Oh, I'm trembling like a leaf," he laughed.

"Wait till I tell you about another Peter," the tall lawyer began. He mentioned that Mrs. Alexander owned an old slave by that name, who was always present at the frequent parties she gave for her many friends and relatives. The slave stood behind her chair, brushing flies off the table with a huge peacock feather. Thus old Peter had heard a great many important conversations.

So Cosby sent a lawyer, Mr. Warrel, to offer the slave a large sum of money, enough to buy his freedom, if he would tell who wrote for Zenger's *Journal.*

Peter was a tall, lean colored man with curly hair already turning gray. Drawing himself up stiffly, he stepped to the door without a word, threw it open, and imperiously showed Cosby's lawyer out.

Within the next three days the faithful old servant had quietly whispered the news in the ears of all the *Journal* writers. They were the leaders of the Popular Party.

"Good for old Peter!" cried Zenger, who always admired loyalty and straight dealing.

There came a loud knock at the door of the shop. Before either of them could go to it, the door was thrown open with a bang, and Sheriff Symes of New York City barged in, followed by the ugly-looking hangman.

The sheriff was not handsome, but Zenger had always liked him. He was a big-boned Dutchman with enormous nose and ears. Though he had marched in brazenly, his manner changed when he caught sight of Mr. Alexander. Suddenly he became humble, took off his leather cap, and nodded. "Excuse us, your Honor. But we got to lay hands on all copies of these numbers of Zenger's paper." He pointed to the handbill, which he was carrying.

Zenger smiled. "Go ahead, search." He opened a big closet. "Here's where we keep old numbers of the paper, all in order. See what you find."

The sheriff and hangman looked in the closet and

also in other parts of the house. But although a few copies of most of the other numbers of the paper were neatly stacked up, none of the ones to be burnt could be seen anywhere.

"Isn't that odd!" Zenger commented. "They were all here yesterday. But now the very numbers you want seem to have disappeared somehow mysteriously."

The sheriff and the hangman grunted and stumped off down the street. Zenger could see them knocking at doors, asking for copies of the papers.

On the morning of the burning Zenger went to a friend's house where, sitting near a window, he could see the pillory.

Judge Harison had taken care that old Mr. Bradford printed plenty of copies of the order for the burning, and that they were tacked up on churches and taverns all over the city. In that town with few public amusements, any kind of show always gathered a crowd.

But the Popular Party had also made its preparations. For one thing, the newly elected aldermen had voted to disobey a special order from the Council for them to attend this burning. They also forbade their hangman to have anything to do with it.

At noon Zenger saw Judge Harison with four of the governor's army officers march out of the City Hall followed by the sheriff and the sheriff's Negro slave. The sheriff carried two or three dozen little newspapers.

The soldiers looked up and down Broad Street and Wall Street. Although this was the lunch hour, when hundreds of laborers usually were strolling about, and this burning had been widely advertised, nobody was in sight.

The two officials shrugged and frowned. They were an oddly contrasting pair. Sheriff Symes, the tall Dutchman, with his homely dull face, huge awkward hands, and sloppy clothes, towered over the brisk, sharp-faced gentleman who wore a pale purple silk suit that had been freshly pressed, and carried a gold-headed cane.

"Well, build a fire!" Harison snapped, flicking down the lace cuffs of his shirt.

Symes protested, "The sheriff can't build a fire with his own hands! It's not dignified!"

"Then order your slave to build one!"

Sheriff Symes turned to his slave. "Fetch some wood, and build us a fire!"

The slave looked about helplessly for kindling and logs and wandered off in search of some. At a near-by carpenter's shop he found a pile of rubbish, mostly chips of wood. As he was gathering an armful, the carpenter stuck his head out the window and bawled, "Thief! Robber! Stealing my wood! Get away from there!"

The poor slave dropped the chips and ran. He met the same answer everywhere. Not one of the shopkeepers would allow even his refuse to be used for such a purpose.

The slave managed to gather enough twigs and paper from the dirty street to start a little blaze.

In a loud voice the sheriff read off the numbers of the *Journals*. "Number 7, ordered to be burned! Number 47, ordered to be burned! Number 48, ordered to be burned! Number 49, ordered to be burned!" He added softly, "Who is to burn them?"

Judge Harison stamped with anger, "Burn them yourself!"

"Hold, Mr. Recorder!" the huge sheriff retorted. "The order of Council says nothing about me. It says the common hangman is to burn them, and he is not here. I do not obstruct the law, but I wish it to be observed that I have no hand in this!" Tossing the papers to the slave, he quickly put his big bony hands behind him and gazed at the sky.

On his way home, Zenger met up with Hendrick Cook, the organist, who had been standing guard at one of the street corners to warn people away, and Nick Sijn, the wheelwright.

"Notice," Hendrick pointed out, "the only person they could find to burn the papers was a slave. He had no choice!"

Nick shook his head. "I do not understand this. Tell me, did not the grand jury refuse to indict Peter Inkpad

or his *Journals* either? And tell me this, has Peter had a trial with a fair hearing and a chance to defend himself and his papers? Or do they do things a more modern way now, begin with the punishment and hold the trial afterward?"

CHAPTER TWENTY-ONE

Zenger Is Caught

THE very next day Zenger's sister Cathie again brought a handbill that was to be posted in all taverns, including hers.

This one was a proclamation signed by Governor Cosby, offering a reward of fifty pounds to anyone who would tell the names of the men who wrote for the *Journal*.

Zenger whistled. "That's a lot of money!"

This offer made him more uneasy than the burning. This reward was something against which he could not fight. Suppose someone did tell—!

Some of the sharpest paragraphs had been written by himself. Others had been by Mr. Alexander, Lewis Morris, Junior, and the other men who had helped Zenger to set up his own shop and to publish a newspaper. What would happen to all of them? If convicted of sedition, they could be hanged.

Trying to conceal from his sister how disturbing her handbill seemed to him, he told her, "Well, nail it up, since you have to. Any old dark corner will do." He followed her to the door of his shop and looked up and down the sunny street, searching in his mind for some joke to make about this proclamation. But for once he could not think of anything funny to say.

Next Sunday, hurrying up Broad Street to play the organ at the old Dutch church, he came face to face with young Chief Justice Delancey.

"Excuse me, your Honor," the Sunday musician begged humbly, almost running into this judge who had commanded a grand jury to indict him.

To Zenger's surprise Delancey smiled. "Ah, Mr. Zenger," he began in a friendly tone. "I have been meaning to speak to you. His Excellency the governor asked me to tell you as a personal message from him that if you will do yourself the good service of letting us know the names of the writers in your *Journal*, he will pay you twice the amount of the reward that has been publicly offered. It is a handsome sum, I believe you will admit, enough for your whole family to live on for some time. Furthermore, he gives you his personal assurance that as a further reward he will guarantee that no harm shall come to you."

Zenger straightened his powerful shoulders, slapped his hat back on his head, and turned to go. As an afterthought he snapped out a quotation from his own paper, "I for one will not sell my friends for a sop and so earn the infamous name of the *sop traitor!*"

Judge Delancey's face turned white with fury.

Zenger marched firmly to his church with his back straight, trying to tell himself that he was not afraid.

The following Sunday—November 17—he and his family walked sleepily home after the long service: first Elizabeth, looking very tiny in a full skirt down to the ground, and with a lace cap over her serious brow; next Nicholas and Pieter, laughing and trying to kick a little stone away from each other, followed by the eldest, John, a quarrelsome boy of eleven. Their parents walked behind. Catherine's prayer book dangled on a chain from her wrist. "After so many threats, nothing has happened to us," she said with a sigh, leaning on her husband's arm.

The shop always seemed unnatural on Sundays. It was so quiet as they herded their little flock into it that the printer stood for a moment staring about at the empty press, the piles of half-finished *Journals* for next day, the cat washing her face under one of the type stands. Catherine shepherded the children into the kitchen out back, where the two babies, Evert and Frederick, were being bathed by her sister, Maria.

When the father was alone, he went over to stroke the cat. He smiled at the printed pages of the City Charter stacked against the wall. Working in all the time he could spare, he had already done about half of it.

"Halt! In the King's name!" boomed a voice behind him so suddenly that he jumped first and then spun around, staring. He recognized John Hendrick Symes, the sheriff.

Two constables, sober workmen like himself, stamped heavily into the shop carrying their six-foot poles, and stood one on either side of him.

"What's going on?" Zenger demanded, more mystified than angry.

The sheriff answered, "You're under arrest!"

The last to enter was Judge Harison, pointing his toes and elbows out and trying to move his arms in an elegant manner under an expensive new blue silk coat and pink neckcloth. But so much anger and violent feeling blazed in his taut face that he seemed not in control of himself. "Read the writ, you blockhead!" he snarled. "And hurry! Someone might come in!"

Sheriff Symes read aloud an order by his Majesty's Council to arrest the printer and put him in jail.

Zenger was not really surprised, but a sudden wave of sadness swept over him. "Well—" he hesitated, "just a minute till I get together a few clothes and say good-bye to my wife. I—"

"Drag him out!" Harison shouted, so choked with rage that his words were scarcely intelligible.

The sheriff spoke to the constables, who seized Zenger's arms.

As they were taking him out the door, Catherine appeared at the other side of the shop. She screamed.

The officers hurried their victim away. They had only a short distance to go, four blocks up Broad Street to the City Hall.

Catherine stood in the doorway of the shop, her children around her, screaming, "Help! Help! They're taking my husband! Help!"

All along Broad Street doors and windows opened. Men and women peered out to see what was happening. It never occurred to poor Zenger to resist the officers, but some of his neighbors came running after them angrily.

Faster and faster the officers hurried, trying to reach the City Hall before the people could be roused enough from their Sunday mood to begin a riot.

All along Broad Street the screams of the printer's sobbing wife followed them.

CHAPTER TWENTY-TWO

Zenger in Jail

ALL afternoon people swarmed noisily outside the locked doors of the City Hall. If the day had not been Sunday, they would certainly have rioted.

Inside, a considerable shifting around was going on. The jail was on the ground floor, with one dungeon in the basement. All types of criminals had to be locked up in the three rooms available—men, women, murderers, thieves, old and young, and also the diseased and insane. Zenger heard some of them shouting, "We don't want to be moved in together!"

After a long wait, he was led down some stairs and thrust into a small, dark, damp, vermin-infested room. The door was locked behind him. When his eyes became accustomed to the darkness, he explored the small space. The floor was covered with straw, where two or three men had been lying. A three-legged stool and a small, battered table were the only furniture. The room was miserably cold.

A couple of hours later a light suddenly appeared through the small speaking hole in the solid wooden door. Looking up quickly, he saw a hand come in holding a tiny stump of a lighted candle. The jailor's voice said, "Take this."

Wondering what next, Zenger hesitatingly took the stub of candle.

"If you want to pay for it, I can send for a dinner for you from a tavern," the jailer offered.

Zenger gave him a paper shilling through the door.

The jailor added, "Kick all that straw into the fireplace and burn it, and I'll bring you some clean straw to sleep on. But don't set fire to the building." This was a sign that the jailor trusted him. Many prisoners had been known to set fire to the building on purpose, and several had escaped that way.

Zenger said earnestly, "I want to send a message to my wife to come and see me."

"She's been here already. We can't let you see her."

"Why not?" Zenger demanded, becoming angry. He knew that a prisoner's wife and family were always let into the jail.

But the jailor answered, "We have orders."

"Then give me pen, ink, and paper!" Zenger demanded. "I want to write to a lawyer!"

"We can't do that either."

Zenger stormed. "You can't deny a prisoner the right to communicate with his lawyer!"

But the man walked away without answering.

"I know where you get those orders!" Zenger shouted after him.

The jailor lived in a room at the head of the stairs. Two bellmen were always on watch. When they went home they were replaced by two others, for the city employed six of them.

In addition to his salary, the city allowed the jailor several small cartloads of fresh straw every month for the prisoners and four shillings a week apiece for food for any who could not feed themselves.

In cold weather the prisoners seldom froze, for if they had no family or friends to bring them wood, the churches sent kindling and logs now and then for charity.

Few prisoners stayed very long. Most of those who were found guilty were hanged—murderers, robbers, thieves, forgers. Those who had stolen only a loaf of bread, both men and women, were taken out and publicly whipped. Often this treatment killed them. But if they survived, they were kept in jail for six months and then set free.

Next morning Zenger heard the clink of the bell which the watchman wore tied to his belt. The door of the cell opened, and the man said, "You're wanted upstairs."

The two guards went with him to a room on the second floor. A sudden feeling of confidence sprang up in him when he found the editor of the *Journal*, Mr. Alexander, and his partner, Mr. Smith. The Court Party called Mr. Smith "the Connecticut mastiff" because they were afraid of him. These two were by far the best lawyers in the whole colony.

"Mrs. Zenger sent me the news," said Mr. Alexander. "I was out of town, but I came as quickly as I could."

"You are a brave man, Mr. Zenger," his partner added, taking the printer's hand and looking him straight in the eye. "We heard about your refusal to reveal our names as writers for your paper—even after your papers had been publicly burned. I like a man with a strong backbone, and we are here to help you."

The poor printer objected, "But I have not enough money to pay one lawyer, much less two!"

Mr. Alexander, the leader of the Popular Party, smiled. "Do not speak of payment, my friend. This is our fight, and if you lose it we shall all be at the beck and call of a tyrant. We can do little, because the judge has already decided against you. But our friend, ex-Judge Morris, who was tyrannously expelled from the office of chief justice of this court, is about to sail for England, where he will personally deliver our appeal to the offi-

146

cials who can give orders to Governor Cosby if they wish. Once before Mr. Morris traveled to London and handed to good Queen Anne a petition against Governor Cornbury, with the result that Cornbury spent a year in this same prison. We can't expect so quick an answer as that from the present King, whose brains are —well!" He coughed. "But we can hope for the best. Meanwhile, if you will sign this paper, giving us authority to help you, Mr. Smith and I will take out a writ of *habeas corpus* and send you home on bail."

With a trembling hand, Zenger signed. Then he was hurried away again to his lonely cell.

Two days later he was again led upstairs to meet his lawyers.

Mr. Smith explained to him, "You must understand, Mr. Zenger, that what is being tried here is not merely a case of one printer. This trial is going to decide whether or not the people of America shall live in freedom under governors who respect the laws, or in slavery under governors who do not."

For the first time since his imprisonment Zenger smiled a little. He liked a good fight, and having two powerful friends on his side was encouraging. "Well," he answered slowly, "if I'm helping other people, I won't mind so much."

Together they went through the door into the courtroom. It was half full of eager townspeople who had

147

come to watch and to try to find the meaning of these frightening events. Judge Delancey, the leader of the Court Party, came in and took his place on the bench. Zenger thought he looked uneasy, in spite of the dignity of his fine clothes and his magnificent, rippling silk wig.

Mr. Alexander, wearing a fresh, short, horsetail wig and a smoother coat than usual, handed the judge a paper called an "exception," stating that Zenger's arrest on an order by his Majesty's Council was illegal. He also said, "I move that the prisoner be released on reasonable bail."

As Judge Delancey read the paper, his face rapidly lost color and his jaw tightened. All he said was, "This exception and the motion for bail may be argued on Saturday in the afternoon."

There was a hurried conference in whispers between Zenger and his lawyers.

Mr. Smith stepped forward in his impressive manner. "Your Honor, my client complains that since he has been confined in the jail, he has been put under such restraint that he has not had the usual liberty of being allowed to have pen, ink, or paper, or to speak with anyone, neither his wife, his friends, nor the minister of the church where he has been the organist. I wish to ask, what authority ordered these secret proceedings? Were they instituted by this court? Or have they been carried out by some other authority in illegal defiance of this court? Is it the intention of this court to—?"

The young judge, glancing uneasily at the angry gentlemen and workmen in the audience, some of whom were rising from their seats in anger, hurriedly interrupted this dangerous tirade of questions. "I understand your complaint, Mr. Attorney. Mr. Sheriff, kindly take note that this court does not countenance the holding of a prisoner incommunicado. The court is adjourned."

Zenger was taken back to the damp, stinking prison.

That afternoon there came a knock at his cell, and a woman's voice called, "Peter!"

Flinging himself against his door, he peered out through the little hole. By the light from the stairs he saw his wife and his tall young son, John.

Eagerly he asked after all the other children. He made arrangements for John to bring food, firewood, blankets, and a warm coat to the jail.

"I'm worried about the *Journal*," he confided. "I won't be home in time to print the next issue. I can't be out of here till Saturday evening, and very likely not then, for where can I get money for bail? The *Journal* was not published the day after my arrest, was it?"

"No," Catherine answered, "my thoughts were all taken up with notifying the lawyers and trying to see you. But I have been thinking of it yesterday and today.

With the help of sturdy John here beside me and our journeyman, who says he will be loyal to us, I think we can publish the newspaper, if you'll give us directions here through the hole in your door."

Zenger cheered. "Hurrah! We'll not let those courtiers silence us!"

"They're going to get a surprise!" Catherine agreed. "But it will mean our setting aside every other work. The City Charter I will stack away in a closet till you are free again. But the *Journal* shall sparkle as brightly as ever!"

"Bring me pen, ink, and paper!" he urged. "I will write for it myself!"

"I will bring them," she promised. "Now the jailor says I may."

CHAPTER TWENTY-THREE

The Fight to Free Zenger

SATURDAY afternoon Zenger was led upstairs to another conference with his lawyers. He was glad to find Catherine there, too. Though she was looking tired and anxious, she held her pretty little chin up, and her eyes looked back at him steadily.

Mr. Smith began, squaring his powerful shoulders, "We do not know how much bail his Honor may demand. As the leader of the Court Party, naturally he would prefer to keep you locked up, to prevent your printing your newspaper. How much bail could you deposit?"

Zenger looked at his wife, and together they made a calculation. Catherine said, "I believe we could scrape together about thirty-eight pounds if we gave all our savings and everything."

Mr. Smith wrote out a statement saying, "I, John

Peter Zenger, am not worth forty pounds, the tools of my trade and wearing apparel excepted."

Zenger read it. "That is true," he commented.

"Then sign it, please." The lawyer explained, "If the judge demands more, even a hundred pounds, I think your friends will lend it to you. The only difficulty is that New York has been having a serious depression for ten years, just as the first pamphlet you ever printed said we would. Although some of our friends own ships, houses, and a good deal of land, they have very little ready cash. And there is no bank in New York, as there is in London, where money can be borrowed."

Zenger shook his head stubbornly. "I am already in debt to those gentlemen. I cannot think of borrowing any more from them."

"Legally you should not need to," Mr. Alexander concluded. "Shall we go in?"

When they passed through the doorway into the courtroom Zenger was amazed at the size of the crowd that had gathered to watch. The historical records say that several hundred of the inhabitants were present. It is hard to believe that so many could have squeezed in, unless they stood all around the walls.

When the two judges had taken their places Delancey announced, "The court will hear the arguments on the question whether the prisoner may be admitted to bail."

Mr. Alexander handed him the signed paper saying that Zenger was not worth forty pounds.

The chief justice glanced at it and grunted, "This is by no means sufficient."

A chill ran through Zenger's chest and shoulders. For a moment the thought of his prison cell rose in his mind, blotting out everything else. He felt its dampness, coldness, darkness. Was he to be locked in it for weeks, awaiting trial?

The lawyers proceeded to argue about the amount of bail. Mr. Alexander began with Magna Carta, quoting the paragraph where reasonable bail is guaranteed to all Englishmen. He mentioned acts of Parliament. The Bill of Rights of 1689 said clearly, "Excessive bail shall never be demanded." Seeing Attorney General Bradley turning the pages of a law book which had several times been quoted in the *Gazette,* Mr. Alexander walked over to him and asked courteously, "Do you mind if I borrow that for a moment?"

The attorney general looked up, startled. "Not at all," he muttered.

Opening to a certain page, Mr. Alexander read aloud.

Zenger's hopes rose as he heard his lawyer prove that in cases of this sort the prisoner must be allowed to go home on bail until the day of the trial.

But Bradley's big fists clenched, and his heavy mouth

became compressed. His opponent was using the Court Party's favorite book against him. Scrambling heavily to his feet, Bradley argued that a libeler arrested by order of his Majesty's Council should not be allowed out on bail at all.

Mr. Smith arose with more facts. When the famous seven bishops had been arrested for libel, just as Zenger was, they had been bailed out at one hundred pounds each. Even an archbishop's bail had been two hundred pounds. Surely a poor printer, not worth forty pounds, should have a lower bail than a bishop.

Bradley leaped to his feet again and shouted, "Who dares compare an archbishop and seven bishops with a stinking, traitorous, sneak thief of a printer, publishing pleas for anarchy in our midst!"

Zenger wanted to get up and smash his fist into Bradley's face. He heard the crowd roaring with anger, booing, hissing, and crying, "Shame on Bradley!" Someone demanded, "Are you an attorney or a bully?"

Mr. Smith, stepping forward in his impressive manner, let fly some of his hammerlike questions, and fairly drowned his opponents in a flood of facts, facts, facts till they shouted and swore. Even the chief justice peevishly joined in the argument, taking sides against Zenger's lawyers. The crowd booed at Bradley and Delancey and cried, "Shame! Shame!"

But Zenger feared that his chances of freedom were lost. Delancey obviously wanted to keep him in jail. He felt again the cold, dark, lonely cell.

The chief justice beat his desk with his gavel, shouting, "Order in the court!" He stared at the heaving multitude of people with a mixture of contempt and fear. When they were reasonably quiet again, he tightened his jaw and angrily announced, "Upon due consideration of all aspects of the case, it is ordered that the prisoner may be admitted to bail, himself in four hundred pounds, with two persons as his sureties, each in two hundred pounds. Until it is given, the prisoner is remanded to jail."

That was it. Zenger slumped in his chair, scarcely noticing the din around him.

Such a roar of booing and stamping burst from the audience that the judges had to march hurriedly away.

Zenger added up the money on his fingers. Eight hundred pounds was more than the value of the whole house and shop that he rented. Even if his patrons offered to lend it, he would be ashamed to accept so much. When Lewis Morris, Junior, had passed the hat and raised fifty pounds for the printing press and type, and again when the gentlemen had advanced a little more to start the newspaper, they had been taking a business risk, which Zenger by hard work could make good to them. But eight hundred pounds! If he accepted this, it would be charity.

He paused in the consulting room with his lawyers only long enough to say, "As that is ten times more than is in my power to give security for to anybody who may offer it, I cannot ask anybody to become my bail on those terms."

Mr. Alexander offered, "Mr. Smith and I are willing to be your sureties and deposit two hundred pounds each, though that is more than we can raise without difficulty. We'll ask your friends if they can collect four hundred for your bail."

"No, no!" Zenger insisted. "I could never accept it!" Sadly, but with his pride intact, he returned to his prison cell.

CHAPTER TWENTY-FOUR

The First Woman Newspaper Publisher

NEVERTHELESS, Governor Cosby's friends pushed back their hats with surprise and grumbled with annoyance on Monday morning, for there came Zenger's two eldest boys running through the streets, shouting, with copies of the newest *Journal*.

It began with a letter from Zenger, written in jail.

The rest of the paper was filled with documents in the case, including one of Judge Delancey's speeches to a grand jury. Some readers were puzzled. "Why does the *Journal* print this speech against it?" asked one of Governor Cosby's friends over a glass of good Madeira wine at Todd's tavern. The Court Party could not understand that they talked like tyrants, and that all Mrs.

Zenger had to do to prove it was to print their own words.

The note at the end still said boldly, "Printed and sold by John Peter Zenger." But the work was managed by Catherine. She kept account of the money. She bought paper and ink. She set type. She read proof. She wrote the foreign news. She taught her children to help more than they had ever done, till Pieter and even Nicholas, seven years old, were setting type. She grabbed the jug of whisky out of the journeyman's hands and made him stay sober till the pages were printed. In short, she was learning how to publish a newspaper.

One December day, while Zenger was talking through the hole in his door to a run-away bond servant and two criminals in the cell at the head of the stairs, a meeting of the new aldermen took place on the second story over his head. He could dimly hear their feet moving about as they entered the courtroom.

By the new City Charter, which he had already partly printed, one half the aldermen (one from each of the seven wards) were judges of the city courts. When they tried a suspected criminal, the recorder (appointed by the governor) sat as chief judge.

One of the seven newly elected aldermen stood up. "Fellow judges of the City of New York, let me call your attention to the fact that two grand juries of this province have in this very room accused the Honorable

Francis Harison, Esquire, recorder of this court, of having committed certain crimes."

Judge Harison, elegantly dressed as usual, spun round in the president's seat and glared at him in horrified astonishment.

The alderman continued, "After these two indictments were presented, his Excellency the governor best knows what became of them." He picked up some papers. "I have here a record of the charges against Mr. Harison, together with copies of the testimony of witnesses who appear to have been victims of outrageous crimes committed by him."

The chief judge leaped up, shaking with fury. "This is an insult! You will never be—"

"We, the elected judges of this city court," the new alderman interrupted sharply, "are not to be silenced by threats!"

Judge Harison struggled to get control of his temper. At last he growled, "It is beneath the dignity of a member of his Majesty's government to take note of such insinuations!" Almost on tiptoe, with rapid, trembling steps he left the room.

The others stared at his back in silence. After a pause they chose one of themselves as vice-president of the court to sit in his place.

The alderman who had been speaking continued, "Fellow judges, I move we call a grand jury of our own, let them see the evidence, and direct them to present their findings to us."

Another asked, "We have control only over city affairs. Is the honorable recorder charged with having broken any city ordinances?"

"Yes, and also with violating the City Charter, which he helped to write. He is charged with having attempted bodily assault against a printer, with having attempted to instigate a riot of sailors and stevedores in a tavern, with having caused one of his servants to beat a man nearly to death, with having led a group of beggars out of this city armed with dangerous weapons and in a warlike manner, with having illegally imprisoned one of his own assistants for a period of nine weeks, a crime that has been proved but for which he has not yet been punished, and with having tampered with the post and intercepted letters addressed to a member of his Majesty's Council, together with other crimes."

After some discussion, they ordered a grand jury to be drawn the next week.

When the city's grand jury met, they seemed frightened by Judge Harison's power, for he was known to be the governor's favorite. The jurors stalled for time. A week passed.

Then all one wintry afternoon during a snowstorm they discussed and argued again. At last they voted to indict him.

The new aldermen met once more. Risking the governor's anger, they wrote a warrant to arrest the honorable recorder of the City of New York and confine him in the common jail.

The city had only one jail, and Zenger was there, waiting.

John Hendrick Symes, the sheriff, accompanied by the same two constables who had arrested Zenger, knocked at the Harison residence. Mrs. Harison, red-eyed from weeping, stood in the doorway with her two little frightened daughters clinging to her skirt, and let the men enter. They searched every room.

Judge Harison was not there.

"Where is he?" asked the sheriff.

"I don't know," she answered truthfully, and sobbed.

Judge Harison had fled. His last known crime was against his own wife and children. He had deserted them. He never even wrote to them again.

Zenger and Catherine discussed this news in whispers through his prison door. Catherine felt bad about it because Mrs. Harison was a Dutch woman, a member of her church.

Zenger, however, was thinking of the possible effect on his own fight against the governor. "I guess anybody who reads our *Journal* must know enough to put the blame for this on Cosby."

Catherine agreed, "Governor Cosby kept him on as editor of the *Gazette* after his crimes were known."

"And tore up at least one indictment against him—maybe two."

"And reappointed him each year to be recorder of the city."

"You know, Catherine, maybe this will teach the governor a lesson. Maybe he'll know better than to keep other crooks to be his helpers, because in the end they only damage his reputation."

CHAPTER TWENTY-FIVE

Judges Under the Governor's Thumb

ZENGER was puzzled by the sudden change in the jailor and the sheriff. Without mentioning the reason, they moved him from the dungeon to a cell on the first floor, which had plenty of daylight and was much easier to keep warm. Although Sheriff Symes was a Court Party man, he began to step into the jail for friendly chats with the printer.

Following the usual custom in English prisons, Zenger's wife and children now began to be allowed to visit him at all times. Once when good old Rip Van Dam quietly sent one of his grandsons over to Mrs. Zenger with a large ham, she cooked it, brought it to the jail, invited the jailor and the other prisoners, and they all gathered in the largest cell for a feast. Thieves, a man who had stabbed another man while drunk, a counterfeiter (whom Zenger had met while working for Bradford), two run-away bond servants, the printer, Catherine, and the children ate together, made jokes, and sang songs till the candles burned out.

If the governor's friends believed they had browbeaten the *Journal* by putting the printer in jail, they were soon disappointed. It came back to the fight with sizzling, stinging attacks against cheating governors who made the judges obey orders.

The *Gazette*, edited now by old Mr. Bradford himself, dropped out of the fight entirely. Its readers had got the habit of writing letters to it, but now Mr. Bradford printed only their advice to the ladies on how to look pretty and suggestions for everyone on how to keep healthy. A couple of letters proposed a law to encourage the farmers to raise more hemp for making rope for the ships. It certainly was not the same paper it had been for the past year.

At the end of January Zenger heard that Attorney General Bradley was again presenting his case to a grand jury. Zenger told the counterfeiter across the hall, "Maybe he figures that the fact of me being here in jail ought to convince 'em that my newspapers contain seditious libels!"

However, the sheriff reported at noon, "Well, Peter,

the grand jury sat on you all morning, but they found nothing against you."

Zenger cheered. He believed he would be set free.

"The judge put it to them pretty strong, too," the sheriff added. "He told them, 'If you find Zenger not guilty, you will be guilty of perjury.' "

That same afternoon Zenger was led upstairs. He met his two lawyers in the little consulting room. Eagerly he asked, "Are they going to let me go?"

Mr. Alexander shook his head sadly, the tail of his short gray wig wagging across his shoulders. "No, Bradley has filed an Information against you."

Zenger dropped with a heavy thump onto a chair. "What on earth is that?"

The lawyer explained. "The attorney general simply writes on parchment his charges against anyone. He calls it an *Information*. And the accused person has to stand trial as though there were a charge against him by a grand jury."

"Is it right for Bradley to be able to do that," Zenger protested, "right after a grand jury has said no?"

Mr. Alexander countered, "When I was attorney general I could force anyone to stand trial on an Information if I so much as happened to dislike the shape of his nose. I never did. But when I retired to practice law, and Bradley took my place, he began to do it."

He sorted his papers restlessly. "Eight years ago, when

our friend Morris, Junior, was a member of his Majesty's Council, he and I wrote a law to prohibit prosecutions by Informations. It was passed by the legislature and is the law today. Unfortunately we left one loophole. We said the attorney general could do it if he could get the signature of the chief justice of the Supreme Court. You remember, Morris's father was chief justice at that time, and it did not occur to us that we might some day be at the mercy of a judge under the thumb of a criminal governor. But that's where we are now; so you have to be tried."

"Now what can we do?" Zenger shrugged in despair. "The judge has already said I'm guilty!"

Mr. William Smith turned to face him squarely and explained in his deep, powerful voice. "I think you already know, Mr. Zenger, that these judges do not have legally correct commissions. They were appointed 'during pleasure,' and Governor Cosby has shown us what that means."

Zenger agreed. "I remember! It means he can kick them out if they decide any case differently from the way he tells them to. That's what he did to old Mr. Morris."

"And you know how Governor Cosby wants your case decided."

Zenger shuddered at this idea. Suddenly he realized what Lewis Morris, Junior, had meant: "When the governor has the judges under his thumb, no one can feel safe." It meant they would hang Zenger. Governor Cosby evidently wanted it, and would order his judges to do it if possible. They would build a new gallows out by Fresh Water Pond on the Common. The cows in the meadow would pay no attention. Perhaps a bird would light on his head after the crowd had gone home. Peter remembered the gallows he had seen when he first arrived in New York.

"Today," Mr. Smith continued, "we are going to offer exceptions to the judges' commissions. We shall argue that judges must not be controlled by any governor."

"Right," said Zenger. "They certainly must not. It's bad for my health!"

CHAPTER TWENTY-SIX

Shall the Judges Be Free?

IN THE courtroom the lawyers presented their exceptions, but Judge Delancey delayed the argument because of a technicality. They must wait till after the vacation.

So Zenger went back to jail for another three months, while the *Journal* kept up the fight.

When they entered the court in April, they again found hundreds of people crowding the room. As the hearing proceeded, Zenger noticed that a number of those present were writing notes on everything that was said. He could feel the excitement among all the spectators.

When the judges were seated, Mr. Alexander began to speak. There was a striking difference between him and Judge Delancey. The tall, awkward lawyer was then forty-three, capable, noted for being a hard worker.

The judge, only thirty, clever but too cocksure ever to open a book, looked proud, pale, and uneasy.

Mr. Alexander began to read from a parchment in his hand. "John Peter Zenger doth take exception to the power of the Honorable James Delancey, Esquire, to judge this case, for these reasons . . ."

Zenger leaned forward a little to listen. His lawyer argued that judges ought to decide each case according to law and justice. But these judges could not do so. Governor Cosby had demonstrated that in this court any judge who disobeyed orders would be dismissed.

Therefore these judges could not legally try Zenger.

The printer, standing within the enclosure called the "prisoner's box," thumped the railing with excited pleasure at this bold challenge. For a moment he glanced around. The crowd had suddenly sat up, looking startled. He thought that many seemed as pleased as he was. He felt the zest of being in a good scrap with plenty of strong people on his side.

Then he glanced back at the judge.

Judge Delancey glowered, puffing with anger. "You and Mr. Smith ought well to consider the consequences of what you are offering!"

"We have considered it carefully, your Honor," Mr. Alexander replied with dignity.

Mr. Smith leaped up, strode powerfully forward, and spoke with even more than usual emphasis. "I, too, your Honor, have carefully considered the consequences of these exceptions. Furthermore, I am so well satisfied of the right of a British subject to take exception to the commissions of two judges, if he thinks such commissions illegal, that I dare venture my life upon that point!"

For just a moment Judge Delancey, the leader of the Court Party, and Mr. Alexander, the leader of the Popular Party, sat eyeing each other in a heavy silence.

Mr. Smith picked up four books. "Will it please your Honor to hear me?"

Judge Delancey answered sarcastically, "We will neither hear nor allow the exceptions! You and your partner thought you would gain a great deal of applause and popularity by opposing this court! But," he added more hotly, suddenly leaning forward, "you have brought it to that point that either we must go from the bench or you from the bar! Therefore we exclude you and Mr. Alexander from the bar!"

Mr. Smith, turning his bull neck, glanced quickly around at Mr. Alexander, wondering if he had heard correctly. There came a universal gasp from the audience.

Turning back toward the judges, Mr. Smith roared, "Never before has an attorney been dismissed for such a cause! This order is sheer tyranny and vengeance!"

Zenger, in amazement, staggered, gripping the railing in front of him for support. He felt as though he had been knocked off his feet. Here he had just been gloating over having the two ablest lawyers in the colony fighting for him. And now suddenly they could not be his lawyers any more. He had no lawyer at all to defend him at his trial.

For the first time in his life he understood what it means to be really afraid. Often he had had little frights. But this was entirely different. They had burned his papers and tried to get a mob to burn down his shop. They had kept him locked for weeks in a cold, damp, lonely prison. And now they left him to flounder alone among these legal tricks, which he did not understand, where he could easily be caught and beaten. It meant, finally, the gallows.

His throat felt dry. His hands on the railing trembled. When he glanced hurriedly around in search of friends, it seemed to him that suddenly most of the faces were hostile.

Then he tried to pull himself together. That snobbish little judge was not going to scare him! Zenger squared his shoulders, stuck his chin out, and glared defiance at both the judges.

The chief justice snapped to the clerk, "Enter this order in the records. The court will recess for ten minutes, while the next case is being prepared."

Both judges marched out of the room.

A Lawyer for Zenger

ZENGER followed Mr. Alexander and Mr. Smith
from the courtroom into the consulting room. Both
slumped down in chairs by the battered old table, their
faces screwed up with perplexity as much as anger.

Zenger was about to speak, but, noticing their expression, he stopped. Abruptly he realized that he was
not the only one in trouble. They were, too. They were
lawyers no more. The work of their whole lives was
suddenly at an end. And they had run this risk defending him.

Mr. Alexander heaved a great sigh. "I must admit
I'm surprised. Such an order has never before been
issued for such a reason in the whole history of the legal
profession. These men are not only tyrants, but they
invent new forms of tyranny!"

The outer door burst open, and Lewis Morris, Junior, rushed in, speechless with indignation. Silently, he gripped Mr. Alexander's hand.

Mr. Alexander shrugged sadly. "Mr. Zenger, I don't know any lawyer in New York whom we can ask to defend you, now that Mr. Smith and I are not allowed to do so. There are only five or six others, and they are all either Court Party men or afraid of Judge Delancey. I suggest you go back into the courtroom now and ask the judge to appoint a lawyer for you."

"Nonsense!" young Morris protested. "If we can't find a good lawyer in New York, we'll hire one from Boston or Philadelphia! We'll get the best attorney in America, and I'll pay his fee myself!"

Zenger turned to Mr. Alexander for advice.

The tall Scot told him, "We'll try. But there may be difficulties. Meanwhile you must have a lawyer. Go on in and ask for one."

When Zenger re-entered the courtroom, with a guard from the jail on either side of him, Delancey was busy with another case. But the judge immediately put it aside and asked Zenger what he wanted.

Zenger gulped with surprise, but the judge smiled encouragement.

"Well, your Honor, I guess I have to ask you to supply a lawyer for me."

Evidently the judge was prepared for this, for he answered at once, "The petition of the accused is accepted. The court appoints John Chambers, Esquire, to serve as your attorney."

A well-dressed lawyer came to shake hands with Zenger.

He, also, was evidently prepared for this, for after a few whispered words with the printer, he said immediately, "My client wishes to enter a plea of *not guilty* to the Information charged against him. If it please your Honor, I move that a date be set for the trial."

Judge Delancey replied, "The case of the attorney general *versus* John Peter Zenger is ordered to be tried Monday, the fourth of August."

Zenger felt some relief in learning at least the exact date.

But, unfortunately, he recognized Mr. John Chambers, who owned a fashionable house on Broadway and had been practicing law for ten years. Mr. Chambers had been a useful alderman for five years, serving as lawyer for the city and helping to write the new City Charter, which Zenger had begun to print. During that wild election, when the Popular Party had fought so hard, Chambers had been a Court Party candidate for re-election and had been defeated 35 to 5. Zenger felt that he must be strongly prejudiced against the man who had printed handbills and even two songs against all the Court Party men. But the printer was forced to depend on Chambers.

Letters came from ex-Judge Morris in London and were quickly passed around among the friends of the Popular Party. Zenger listened eagerly when Catherine read them to him in the jail, hoping that that powerful and clever man in England could rescue him by having Governor Cosby called home.

But Mr. Morris had written glumly, "We have a parliament and cabinet ministers, some of whom, I am ready to believe, know there are colonies and governors. But they are as unconcerned at the sufferings of the people in America as we are at those of crows and king-fishers."

During the weeks after Mr. Chambers was appointed to be Zenger's lawyer, the poor prisoner knew that friends were busy trying to get him a better one. But Catherine had to confess in his cell, "They wrote to a Mr. John Kinsey in Philadelphia, but he answered that Governor Cosby has done him some favors; so he feels it would be impolite for him to serve as your lawyer in this case." She sighed. "However, we shall keep on trying."

"So I am to be defended by an enemy!" Zenger exclaimed bitterly. Thrusting his hands into his pockets, he paced broodingly across his cell.

Catherine, seated on a three-legged stool, looked up. "Even Mr. Chambers may be useful to us. Don't forget, he is a lawyer, and if he wins a case—any sort of case—

he gains prestige. I think he may try. Also, there is something else."

Feeling a little spark of hope, Zenger turned toward her inquiringly.

She continued, "I don't know that he is really a strong Court Party man. His defeat in the election of aldermen last summer was a heavy blow to him. He told me, 'It was a big surprise to me to learn how unpopular Governor Cosby has been.' "

Zenger asked hesitatingly, "You don't suppose we could win him over?"

She stood up, smiling a little. "Peter, I believe the real reason Mr. Chambers followed the Court Party was that he thought it consisted of the most wealthy and influential people. When I told him who some of the Popular Party men are and how much land and how many servants they own, he looked very thoughtful."

Zenger's eyes opened wide.

"And when I whispered to him behind my hand that Mr. Alexander is a cousin of the Earl of Stirling and will be heir to the title, he ran right off to ask his advice!"

Zenger laughed. "Keep it up! If we can turn one enemy into a friend, we'll at least be good Christians, even if it doesn't save me from being hanged."

CHAPTER TWENTY-EIGHT

First Test of the New Lawyer

THE long weeks of waiting passed slowly for Zenger in the jail. All his knowledge of printing, his skill in setting type and working the press, were idle, useless. Restlessly he paced his cell, sometimes beating the walls in a frenzy of boredom, longing for something to do. His heavy muscles began to soften from disuse.

As spring came he sagged at the window, clutching the bars, gazing at the new, sprouting leaves. On warm days he smelled Mr. Bayard's sugar mill not far away. He was glad whenever a fire occurred, for then he could hear the men running and shouting, pulling out the new fire engines, which were housed in the room next to his prison cell.

On Wednesday, July 16, sudden death came close to him. On that day Governor Cosby gave a huge picnic to celebrate the completion of the foundations of "the new battery on Whitehall Rocks." (The place has been called the Battery ever since that day.) The governor, the Court Party members of his Majesty's Council, and many of the "principle gentlemen and merchants of this city" went out to lay the cornerstone of the upper platform. Speeches were made, flags were waved, and the old rusty cannon fired salutes.

A crowd gathered to watch and to eat. At a wooden booth especially built near by, the governor and his friends ate a dinner, while a whole ox, barbecued over a huge fire, was provided free by the governor to the "workmen, laborers, and people—with several barrels of punch and beer."

Everybody was happy. Even the Popular Party had asked for this new battery to protect New York in case of war. But the *Gazette* reported:

Upon the conclusion of the solemnity, when his Excellency was returning in the manner he went [in a parade] and the last round was firing, the very last cannon, being very much honey-combed with rust and eaten almost through, burst. And the fragments of it, flying different ways, killed three persons.

The three victims were a child, a young gentleman, and John Hendrick Symes, the sheriff.

Catherine Zenger wrote the sheriff's death notice in the *Journal:*

179

As to his character, I think that the unanimous wishes of the inhabitants of this city to have his place supplied with another like him, speak louder than anything I can attempt.

As he was the officer who had arrested Zenger, this was an extraordinary tribute.

Late in July came the first test of the new lawyer, Mr. Chambers.

At five o'clock one hot afternoon Zenger was led upstairs from the prison to the courtroom for the drawing of a jury. He was glad to find a dozen of his friends, including Lewis Morris, Junior, Fred Bekker, Hendrick Cook the organist, Nick Sijn the wheelwright, and old Rip Van Dam, who was still president of his Majesty's Council even though Governor Cosby never let him know when it was meeting.

Attorney General Bradley, his heavy brows drawn down sternly, came in late, smiling to himself about something. But the judges were away.

When Zenger sat at a long table beside his handsomely dressed lawyer, he noticed that Mr. Chambers smelled of soap and expensive wig powder. Zenger frowned at him suspiciously. Mr. Chambers, who smiled pleasantly, was probably already plotting to betray him, he thought.

Death had complicated Zenger's problem. The custom, as he had explained in his *Journal,* was for a panel of forty-eight possible jurors to be copied by the sheriff from the voters' book, and the jury of twelve would later be chosen from these forty-eight. But now there was no sheriff. In this hot weather Governor Cosby was resting on the seashore in New Jersey and had not yet appointed one.

So the responsibility fell on the sloping shoulders of the court clerk, a stiff, precise man named James Lyne. He was also a surveyor. His map of New York, printed by Mr. Bradford some years before, was excellent.

Mr. Chambers told him, "We are ready to proceed with striking the jury."

The clerk, evidently feeling important, as he was running the court while the judges were away, pompously drew out a large sheet of paper and began reading names from it in his astonishingly loud voice.

Zenger listened carefully, because here was his one chance of escape from death. Since the judge had already called him guilty, his only hope was his jury.

He heard the names with increasing horror. The clerk's list consisted of guards at the fort, customs inspectors, and others holding jobs under Governor Cosby during his pleasure. Some were not voters at all. Cosby's baker was listed, his tailor, his shoemaker, his candlemaker, his carpenter, his stablekeeper, and several of the former aldermen who had been defeated in the last election largely because of what Zenger had printed against them.

Without even noticing his own lawyer, Zenger turned to appeal to his friends. But he saw that Lewis Morris had already leaped up and was pointing an accusing finger at Attorney General Bradley, who sat studying a list of his own. "The attorney general there, so I've been told by someone who is likely to know, has a list in his hand of the few unbiased men in this so-called jury panel and is ready to strike them out!"

Suddenly Bradley stopped smiling. In great embarrassment, he quickly stuffed his list in his pocket.

At this, Mr. Chambers obviously had to do something for his client. Rising to his feet, he looked around to see what the group of men seemed to expect of him.

After one glance at all their grim faces, the lawyer coughed and spoke formally, "Mr. Clerk, on behalf of my client, I must request that you bring out the voters' book and choose from it forty-eight qualified jurors in our presence, as usual."

Zenger clapped his hands together, silently cheering. Reaching forward, he tugged the lawyer's coat to catch his attention, and whispered, "Good work! Keep it up!"

The clerk, becoming angry, insisted, "I have the list here!" He smoothed with his hand the paper which he himself had written.

In this crisis Zenger's new lawyer stood uneasily looking around at the faces that stared at him from all sides.

At last Mr. Chambers said, "Mr. Clerk, you will have to apply to their Honors the judges at tomorrow's sitting of the court."

Zenger sprang up with delight and clapped his lawyer on the shoulder to congratulate him. Mr. Morris and Mijnheer Van Dam also hurried forward to shake his hand and wish him well.

Next morning Zenger came anxiously between his two guards into the courtroom. Rumors of this new scandal about the false jury panel must have spread, for a much larger number of people had gathered. All the shopkeepers from Zenger's neighborhood were sitting grimly on the benches, watching and waiting. They knew that if Zenger were hanged by the Court Party's trickery, their lives would be unsafe, too, for they could never speak or print the truth freely again.

Mr. Chambers stood up and explained apologetically to the judges what the clerk had done the previous afternoon.

An angry growl burst from the whole crowd.

Zenger's lawyer seemed to enjoy the fact that he was important, now that the real fight had begun. He glanced at Zenger, who whispered, "Keep on! Keep on!"

Putting one foot forward and stuffing two fingers between the buttons of his handsome, brocaded waistcoat, the lawyer added more firmly, "I move that a panel of forty-eight jurors be copied out of the voters' book as usual in the presence of both parties."

Judge Delancey cleared his throat and looked around the room. Almost a hundred faces glared back at him threateningly. Zenger waited in suspense. After a pause the judge said in a voice so low it was scarcely audible, "The motion is granted."

Zenger nodded approval to Mr. Chambers, who followed up his success immediately. "And I move that the clerk hear objections to the persons proposed to be of the forty-eight, and allow such objections as are just."

"Granted," muttered the judge. He seemed to be angry because he could not refuse.

Zenger's back straightened slowly, and he began to breathe again. Now that his jury was going to be chosen from a group of men picked at random from among the voters, there was a good chance that he might get men who would try him fairly.

As the two guards began to march him away, he paused long enough to grip the lawyer's hand and thank him.

"I've heard important news," Mr. Chambers whispered. "I can't tell you more just now, but you have other friends at work besides these here in this room."

What did he mean? Zenger was puzzled. At least it was a partial explanation of his lawyer's friendly attitude. It meant that somebody else had been talking or writing to Mr. Chambers and had persuaded him to treat his client well. Who could it be?

As Zenger was hurried out of the room by his two guards, he held his shoulders firmly, for he felt at last that he had a fighting chance.

CHAPTER TWENTY-NINE

The Purpose of Juries

IN HIS prison cell Zenger sat at a table littered with papers. He was hard at work, a quill pen gripped between his teeth, his sleeves rolled up, bits of ink in his hair where he had run his fingers through it.

Secure under the inkwell was the proof sheet of the most important article for next week's *Journal*. In his left hand was a letter he himself had written. Scattered in front of him were news reports from Europe and seventeen letters from friends who wanted to help him. He could not possibly find room for all this material in one newspaper.

He shoved everything else aside and picked up the proof sheet from under the inkwell. Mr. Alexander, as editor of the paper, had said he could not approve of

this feature article until he had consulted his partner, William Smith. Zenger was expecting them at the prison any minute.

Zenger began to read the article again, loudly tapping the fingers of his right hand on the table. Then he jumped up and paced the floor. Every time he ran his eyes over these sentences he became too excited to sit still.

Lewis Morris, Junior, had sent in the article neatly copied in his father's handwriting. It had just arrived in a letter from London. Carefully inscribed across the first page was the title of a book from which it was supposed to have been taken. But Zenger suspected that ex-Judge Morris might have written it himself, for it sounded like the style of some humorous articles he had written the previous year.

It was a dialogue about the duties and privileges of jurymen, and a citizen's rights under Magna Carta. Often, lately, Peter Zenger had thought of Magna Carta, but today it had new meaning. He thought of it as he pondered his own court problem:

Judge Delancey was going to tell the jury that they could decide only the fact, whether the accused did or did not print the newspapers. Well, obviously Zenger had, of course. The other question, whether the papers were seditious libels, was a matter of law, the judge would say, which they must leave to him. And the judge had already decided that the papers were.

The only way Zenger could possibly be saved would be for the jury to decide both questions. Would the jurors have the courage to do it?

When he heard the jailor unlocking his door, he hurried to set the chair and stool both by his table, and to put the papers in order.

Mr. Alexander stooped to pass under the lintel. Peter noticed that both he and his broad-shouldered partner looked troubled as they greeted him.

Mr. Smith's shoulders twitched with irritability, probably because his great talent for the law would have to lie unused. To support his large family he would have to take up some business, which he disliked. He had been closing his office, bringing to an end all his law practice.

Mr. Alexander was taking the blow a little more easily, but his face was seamed with downward-pointing lines. Both men were in a fighting mood.

"In the first place," Zenger began, standing humbly while the two lawyers sat down to look over the papers, "my wife can't finish the *Journal* on Monday—the day of my trial—because the court has subpoenaed our journeyman and our two eldest sons for that day to be witnesses against me." He came closer. "But if the governor's friends think they can quiet us that easily, let them think again!"

Mr. Alexander looked up. "What do you propose to do?"

"Bring the paper out this Saturday instead," Zenger offered. "We'll let my whole jury panel have a chance to read it before the trial begins."

"That's good strategy," the editor agreed. "But I have some doubt about this article on the duties of jurymen." He tapped the proof sheet on the table.

"If Judge Delancey has his way," Zenger demanded, "what use is a jury? I might as well be tried without one!" He slapped the proof sheet, too. "Either the jurors must do what this article says, or I'm a dead man!"

Mr. Smith suddenly entered the discussion. "And if you are hanged, the press in America will be choked for a hundred years!"

"Aye," the editor answered, "but we don't want to cheat by printing any false statements."

Mr. Smith shook his head. "Certainly not!"

Mr. Alexander hesitated, leaning forward to peer at the article again. "If we print this, it will be the most effective move we shall have made in the whole case." He looked his partner in the eyes. They were honest eyes. "Tell me, my friend. Just among friends, is this article good law?"

Mr. Smith opened his mouth to answer, then closed

it. His face was very sober, almost frightened. After a moment he began again, "When you say, 'good law,' you mean, of course, law as it has been practiced up to now."

"Yes."

"Then this is my answer." This sturdy man, who knew more about law than anyone else in New York, stood up and walked across the room before he gave his opinion. "My friend, you and I know that this is not exactly 'good law' as practiced up to now. But—" he turned and raised one clenched fist, "this is human justice as my conscience tells me God intended it to be!"

Mr. Alexander leaped up and gripped his hand. "I will stand by you on that with every ounce of strength I possess!" He picked up the article and handed it to Zenger. "Go ahead and print it."

The article was in the form of a conversation between a lawyer and a juror:

The lawyer told him, "What a judge may or may not do is carefully prescribed in the laws. For example, he cannot refuse to accept the jury's verdict when the jury has agreed on it."

Then the lawyer asked him, "Suppose you were a juror in a case where a man is accused of being a false *traitor* because he walked with his hat on in front of a picture of the King. And suppose that sufficient witnesses should swear to the fact, namely, that he did pass by the picture with his hat on. Now imagine yourself one of the jury that were sworn to try him. What would you do?"

"Do?" answered the juryman. "Why, I should be satisfied in my conscience that the man had not committed any crime."

"You speak as an honest man," the lawyer complimented him.

"But," the juryman added in much perplexity, "the judge has said, leave the law to him. Truly it is somewhat hard, and I pity the poor prisoner, but we cannot help it. We must bring in a verdict of *Guilty* for the fact, and leave the judge to say what the law provides for him."

"God protect every honest man from such jurymen!" cried the lawyer. "Have you more regard for the judge than for justice? By your oath you swear, 'I will well and truly try the prisoner and a true verdict make.' That means, upon your conscience and the best of your understanding. If you are satisfied that the man has committed no crime, what can you do but acquit him? For the purpose of juries is to protect men from oppression!"

CHAPTER THIRTY

The Trial Begins

PROMPTLY at nine o'clock on the morning of August 4, 1735, when Zenger was led into the courtroom by his lawyer and his two guards, he found the young judges Delancey and Philipse already seated in their places. They were wearing their finest wigs and most impressive suits as though for a specially important ceremony.

Mr. Chambers, the lawyer, also was wearing a splendid new suit of brown silk damask for the occasion. Old Rip Van Dam, Lewis Morris, Junior, Mr. Smith, and several other leaders of the Popular Party quickly clustered near him and whispered advice or eyed him sternly. Mrs. Zenger tried to touch her husband's hand as he passed, but although he held out his arm he could not quite reach her.

Taking his place in the prisoner's box, he looked

around at the noisy, shuffling crowd. For a moment he felt as important as an actor about to make a dramatic speech. Then he began to look more carefully.

The forty-eight men of the jury panel were waiting expectantly in the audience on the left. Crowded on the right there waited a number of Governor Cosby's friends, who seemed puzzled as they peered about. They probably wondered why so many people were interested. Surely the trial would be very simple. The jury would decide that Zenger had printed the papers. The judges would decide that the papers were libelous and seditious. The hangman would do the rest.

Zenger smiled. Now that he had reached the last day of his long fight, he was no longer afraid. He had strong friends—though he was a little disturbed not to see the most important one. Mr. Alexander was so tall, his head would have showed if he had been anywhere in the room. But Zenger was ready to tell the judges that he would print the truth openly—about governors or judges or anyone—or die in the attempt, and then let the jury decide.

He glanced again at the men of the jury panel, hoping that they had read the article in his latest *Journal*.

He drew courage from the look in his wife's intelligent eyes as she gazed back at him. Among the spectators he found his sister and her husband with their

oldest boy and two of his children, little Elizabeth and
Nicholas.

He was worried when he did not see his older boys,
John and Pieter, but he supposed they were in the witness room. Farther back he discovered other relatives,
his brothers and sisters-in-law, who waved to him and
tried to offer him their courage by the way they raised
their fists and smiled.

As he exchanged glances with all these sturdy people
who meant so much to him, and saw clearly in their
strained, anxious faces how much they cared about him,
he began to wish he could win the trial for their sakes.
The jury's decision would either bring him home to
them or send him away forever.

Scowling at the judges, who both looked very young
to him—almost as young as his sister—he could see
what they wanted. Let him be cruelly punished, and
then no other printer—perhaps ever again—would be
able to print the truth. As he turned toward his old
friend Mijnheer Van Dam, whom he had once saved
from jail by a pamphlet, Zenger wondered if today's
trial would let him again protect anyone by means of
his press. Or would he be sent off finally to jail or the
gallows, his press forever silenced, so that corrupt government officials could rob or imprison anyone as they
pleased? He wrung his strong hands, aching with the

wish to win this trial and be able to fight them again tomorrow.

He had noticed that a hush had spread over the crowded benches when he had appeared. Hundreds of faces were now watching him anxiously. The sheriff stood up to speak.

In the sticky summer heat Governor Cosby had lazily neglected to appoint a new sheriff for New York. But his son, Billy Cosby, began the trial. Billy, a short, fat, rosy-complexioned young man, was sheriff of Perth Amboy in New Jersey. Now it seemed he had been sent over to summon the jurors in this trial and hand in their names to the court.

Zenger glared, feeling sure that that plump young man was going to try in some way to pack the jury. Catching the eye of his own lawyer, Zenger signaled to him to be on his guard, for the jury was their only hope.

Mr. Chambers stepped forward and said smugly, "I humbly move your Honors that we may have justice done by the sheriff, and that he may return the names of the jurors in the same order as they were taken from the book."

Judge Delancey sat up with a start. When Mr. Chambers proved that the list of jurors' names had been twisted around, the young judge's pale cheeks flushed. An angry murmur rippled through the audience.

Each minute more people were entering through the doorway.

Zenger glanced again at the forty-eight jurors waiting on the left side of the room. Had they understood this hint? He was pleased to notice that some were shaking their heads and that others were whispering to their neighbors. Perhaps they had already been swayed in his favor. Zenger smiled.

Noticing his smile, Judge Delancey hurriedly tried to cover up this damage to the Court Party's cause, and with a great show of being fair, ordered the list of names to be set right.

As soon as the judges had given in, a sigh, accompanied by some titters, came from the crowd. By now no empty seats were left, and late comers had to stand.

One by one, as the men of the jury panel were called, they walked forward to the jury box and were questioned by Attorney General Bradley and by Mr. Chambers, who proved to be not only clever, but also a good talker.

After questioning each one, Mr. Chambers glanced at Zenger. Zenger shook his head if he thought the juror was prejudiced against him. Then Mr. Chambers made a challenge, and the juror was dismissed. When a man seemed unbiased, Zenger nodded, and Mr. Chambers announced, "The juror is acceptable to the defendant."

Zenger cheered silently. However, when he smiled

too much at one juror, a friend of his, Attorney General Bradley immediately made a challenge, and the judge snapped, "Juror dismissed!"

Zenger swore silently.

The ones who were accepted by both sides were told to stand up in the jury box.

The clerk asked in his loud voice, "Do you solemnly swear that you will well and truly try John Peter Zenger, the defendant, and a true verdict make, so help you God?"

Each juror, with his hand on the Bible, answered, "I do."

Zenger noticed that it was the same oath his *Journal* had claimed it would be.

He glanced around. Several copies of his newspaper, containing these words, lay on the floor where the jurors had been sitting in the audience before they were called. He was so excited that he made signs to his wife to call her attention to the rumpled papers, but she signaled back to him to be quiet.

At last twelve jurors were accepted. Zenger stared at them. The foreman, Thomas Hunt, was a sturdy man whose face did not tell what he might be thinking. But seven—a majority—were of Dutch ancestry and attended the church where Zenger was organist. And at least one of them, Herman Rutgers, had served on that first grand jury a year and a half before, which had refused to indict Zenger on this same charge of libeling, in spite of Judge Delancey's passionate speech to them at that time demanding that they do so. Zenger began to be hopeful.

More and more people were arriving to watch this important trial. They filled all the seats, stood three deep around the walls, sat bunched together on the sills of all the open windows, stood crowded in the doorway and on the stairs outside. He could hear others in the street below.

A disturbance at the doorway drew everyone's attention. Zenger at last saw Mr. Alexander's friendly face towering above the crowd, looking pleased and important. With some difficulty the men squeezed back and let him pass.

Beside him walked a dignified old gentleman in a long, curled, formal wig such as the wealthiest courtiers wore. Slowly these two newcomers made their way down the center aisle together, for the old man limped badly and seemed to be in very poor health.

Zenger turned anxiously to his friends to learn the meaning of this. His wife was evidently very much excited, bouncing up and down in her seat and pressing her little fist against her mouth.

Slowly, painfully, the old gentleman and Mr. Alexander made their way to the front of the courtroom, followed by two servants carrying books.

Clerk Lyne demanded in his loud voice, "What name did you say?"

The old gentleman evidently answered, for the clerk repeated loudly after him, "Andrew Hamilton, Esquire," and wrote it down. Then the clerk asked, "Where were you admitted to the bar?"

By this time everyone was listening breathlessly. Old Mr. Hamilton answered in a clear, firm voice, "In London, by a special commission from her Majesty, Queen Anne."

As he limped over to shake hands with Zenger, a crescendo of eager whisperings swept the crowded room.

Mr. Alexander hurriedly whispered to the poor printer, "We didn't dare tell you sooner. My wife traveled secretly to Philadelphia in her yacht to persuade this gentleman to defend you, and they returned only this morning. His health was so poor, we were afraid that if we told you we should only get your hopes up and then he might not be able to make the trip."

Judge Delancey was glowering from the bench. The friends of Governor Cosby gasped and whispered angrily to one another, for evidently Mr. Hamilton was well known to them. Mr. Alexander hurriedly explained to Zenger that for ten years Mr. Hamilton had been a distant partner of his in important cases that reached beyond New York. And even before that, Mr. Hamilton had defended the government of New York in a suit for unpaid taxes here in this very court. He had been William Penn's lawyer and was a close friend of Benjamin Franklin. He had been attorney general of Pennsylvania, recorder of the city of Philadelphia, and a member of the Pennsylvania legislative assembly. For the past six years he had been speaker (or president) of that assembly.

But, as Zenger could see, he appeared to be nearly eighty years old and was badly afflicted with the gout.

He took his seat beside Mr. Chambers. Zenger had started the trial with two lawyers. Now again he had two.

Nervously eyeing the newcomer, Attorney General Bradley consulted his assistant, then stood up, cleared his throat, and began the accusation. Holding the Information high in his big hand, he began to read in a dramatic manner.

The long sentences full of legal terms almost put Zenger to sleep, till suddenly in the midst of them he heard Bradley loudly reading paragraphs from his newspaper. The familiar slashing, stinging phrases, which Zenger himself had set up in type and had printed on his creaking wooden press, made the whole courtroom sit up. It sounded strange to hear Governor

Cosby's own lawyer reading those paragraphs, which plainly called Governor Cosby a tyrant and a criminal who broke the laws and tried to enslave the people.

Zenger glanced quickly around the room. He could not help feeling some satisfaction that he had not only printed these attacks against an evil governor, but he had also made the attorney general read them aloud to the largest crowd ever seen at the Supreme Court of New York.

The effect on the listeners was not what the attorney general intended. Zenger could see many of them nodding their heads in agreement with the words he had printed. Zenger smiled.

During all this reading, the aged Mr. Hamilton and Mr. Alexander were busily whispering with Zenger's other lawyer, Mr. Chambers.

Mr. Chambers came over to consult the prisoner, then carried his words back to Mr. Hamilton.

By the time Bradley had finished and sat down, Zenger's lawyers were ready.

Mr. Chambers began the defense. Bowing politely to the jury, he explained very clearly what the word *libel* meant. "It is any statement published with malicious purpose to expose somebody to public hatred or ridicule."

Zenger listened anxiously, for he did not fully trust this man who was defending him. But Mr. Chambers had been studying the subject for the past three months, and seemed eager to show his learning. Also he was a smooth talker and knew well how to influence a jury. With a glance at Mr. Hamilton, he concluded by saying merely, "I am in hopes that Mr. Attorney General will fail to prove that those paragraphs are libels."

Mr. Alexander taking one arm and Mr. Chambers the other, they helped Mr. Hamilton to his feet. Zenger was in despair. He was impressed with Mr. Hamilton's many titles, but was his life going to depend on this feeble old invalid, who probably knew very little about his case?

CHAPTER THIRTY-ONE

The Cause of Liberty

THE elderly lawyer limped forward one step. Zenger was slightly relieved when he saw how firmly he squared his shoulders and raised his fine, handsome head. "May it please your Honors, I am concerned in this cause on the part of Mr. Zenger, the defendant. In the common course of proceedings, Mr. Attorney General would be called upon to prove that my client printed and published those newspapers. But I cannot think it proper for me to deny his having published complaints which I think are the right of every free-born person to make. And therefore I'll save Mr. Attorney General the trouble of examining his witnesses to that point. I do, for my client, confess that he both printed and published the two newspapers quoted in the Information. And I hope in so doing he has committed no crime."

There was a gasp from the Court Party men in the audience. Since the jury had nothing to decide but the question of whether Zenger had or had not printed these things, this confession ended the trial. The judges could now dismiss the jury and decide the other question themselves, that is, whether the paragraphs were or were not libels.

Attorney General Bradley leaped heavily to his feet. Spluttering with excitement, he burst out, "Then if your Honor pleases, since Mr. Hamilton has confessed the fact, I think our witnesses may be discharged. We have no further occasion for them."

Mr. Hamilton turned on him with a dramatic sweep of his arm, as though brushing the attorney general and all his friends away. He exclaimed boldly, "If you brought them here only to prove the printing and publishing of these newspapers, we have acknowledged that and shall abide by it!"

Zenger, sticking his chin out at the judges, nodded in vigorous agreement.

A murmur of excited whisperings spread over the room. Many of the men half rose from their chairs, waiting to hear if Judge Delancey would dismiss the jury. Gradually silence returned and became so intense that Zenger could hear the breathing of the people around him.

There was much whispering back and forth among

Bradley, the clerk, and Sheriff Billy Cosby. Zenger's journeyman and his two sons, John and Pieter, followed by several neighbors, were led in from the witnesses' room. The clerk told them in his loud voice that they were no longer needed. They crowded over to the side of the room, looking for places where they could stand.

Zenger was relieved to see his boys at last. He was not disturbed about their being witnesses against him, for if they had had a chance to speak up on the witness stand, he knew they would both have told the truth about him and been proud of it, as Mr. Hamilton had just done.

They waved to him. In their pleasure at seeing their father they did not seem to care about the huge crowd of people watching them.

The young judge waited impatiently. At last he said, "Well, Mr. Attorney General, will you proceed?"

A sigh of satisfaction came from the crowd. The jurymen looked at one another and smiled. The judge did not dare risk trying to dismiss them.

Attorney General Bradley was obviously rattled. He raised his hands and let them flap helplessly against his legs as he spluttered. But when Zenger and the jury really began to believe that he was caught off guard and was not prepared, Bradley recovered himself. He swept up a thick pile of papers from his table and held them

high for all to see, to prove that he was thoroughly prepared.

He talked convincingly. But every argument he set up, Mr. Hamilton tried to knock down. Were Zenger's paragraphs libels or not? The lawyers fought over this question. Sometimes they seemed like two gentlemen with fencing swords. But more often Zenger felt that they were going at each other like two thugs with heavy clubs.

Bradley said that governors and other government officials had to be respected, else people would not obey them. Therefore any printed statement attacking a governor was libel, and the printer must be punished.

Mr. Hamilton made fun of that. When people suffer from the cruel and unjust acts of a governor, don't they have a right to complain? How can the mere printing of a true complaint be libel? And he offered to call witnesses to prove that the statements printed by Zenger were true.

The printer, standing wearily in the hot courtroom, smiled at this offer. It would be fun to watch witnesses stand up here and prove that Governor Cosby really had stolen 50,000 acres of land, really had denied Mijnheer Van Dam the right of trial by jury, really had accepted bribes, really had cheated in two elections, and all the rest of what the *Journal* had been saying.

Frightened by this offer, Judge Delancey joined in

the argument and bickered with the aged lawyer. The judge even claimed that it made no difference whether the statements printed by Zenger were true or not. If they were against the governor, that was enough. That made them libels.

Mr. Hamilton was too clever for him. He tore down the judge's arguments and made the judge look silly.

But Judge Delancey had to obey the orders of Governor Cosby. Never mind what the law said. He could not allow witnesses to prove that those statements about Cosby were true. If the judge permitted such a thing, he would, he knew, instantly be dismissed by the governor. So he ordered Mr. Hamilton to stop arguing with him.

Mr. Hamilton then turned dramatically to the jury. "Gentlemen, it is to you we must appeal. You easily can guess why the court will not allow us to call witnesses. Everyone in New York knows now whether these statements about the governor are true or not."

The fight continued until Zenger was so tired that he only wished they would stop talking and let him sit down.

Attorney General Bradley quoted old trials in the law books, where printers had been punished, saying that Zenger's case must be decided the same way.

Mr. Hamilton began to read other cases to prove that, on the contrary, it was no crime to print true complaints against a governor, and that the jury could decide both the fact and the law and find Zenger *not guilty*.

Mr. Alexander was kept busy hopping up every two minutes to bring Mr. Hamilton another book. Mr. Smith and Mr. Chambers began to look like overworked librarians, feverishly keeping track of the volumes piled high on the table, on chairs, and on the floor.

At the end Mr. Hamilton rose to great eloquence. "The question before the court and you, gentlemen of the jury, is not of small nor private concern. It is not the cause of the poor printer, nor of New York alone, which you are now trying. It may in its consequences affect every freeman in America. It is the best cause. It is the cause of liberty!"

A hush came over the room as Mr. Alexander and Mr. Chambers helped the aged attorney to return slowly, painfully to his chair. The whole crowd seemed to realize that they were in the presence of a great event.

The aged lawyer from Philadelphia had fought so dramatically and so cleverly that this trial was the origin of a popular expression used for many years afterward: "as smart as a Philadelphia lawyer."

In conclusion Attorney General Bradley walked over to the jury and made an extraordinary admission. Boastfully he announced, "It is the opinion of his Excellency our governor and his Majesty's Council that

Mr. Zenger ought not to be allowed to go on disturbing the peace of the government by publishing such libels against his Excellency our governor and against the chief persons in the government. Therefore his Excellency himself, by and with the advice of the Council, has directed this prosecution."

Zenger gave a start when he heard this. In other words, Governor Cosby did not want newspaper readers to know what he was doing, and he was going to stop that paper if he could. The question being tried was at last perfectly clear. Did newspapers have the right to let the people know what the government officials were doing? Or did the governors have the power to act secretly, as they pleased, and to punish anyone who complained?

Finally young Judge Delancey turned and gave his instructions briefly and angrily to the jury, telling them bluntly to find Zenger *guilty* and be quick about it.

The twelve jurors, looking self-conscious under the great responsibility that had been put on them, marched out to their own consulting room.

Zenger's two guards led him out the rear door and down the back stairs to the jail. He would not have much longer to wait in suspense.

The Verdict

ZENGER flopped onto his little pallet of straw, exhausted after having stood on his feet in the courtroom for five hours.

He had no idea what the jury would do. They had been instructed to find him *guilty* as to the fact, and leave the rest to the judges. Finding him *not guilty* of having printed and published "false, malicious, seditious libels" would be an open defiance of the judge's orders, and the jurors might be jailed for it, for contempt of court—if Judge Delancey so ruled. And he might well do so, for he enjoyed the position he held at the pleasure of Governor Cosby.

When the printer had been lying on the straw about ten minutes, the door of the cell opened and the jailor entered.

Zenger sat up sleepily. "I guess I'd better have some lunch."

"You're wanted upstairs. The jury's back."

"Already?" Zenger scrambled to his feet.

He found the courtroom jammed tighter than ever with eager, anxious people. Through a window he heard the increasing noise of the excited crowd in the street below.

The foreman, Thomas Hunt, stood facing the judge. Delancey glared back at him.

The slim clerk stood up and asked in his loud voice, "Gentlemen of the jury, have you agreed upon a verdict?"

The foreman answered just as loudly, "We have! *Not guilty!*"

Before Zenger could really take in the verdict, he heard someone sob. Then he saw his wife jump to her feet with a smile on her face and tears streaming down her cheeks.

He saw almost the whole crowd leap up, waving their arms and shouting "Hurrah!" Judge Delancey opened his mouth to say something. It was drowned in another "Hurrah!" and then another.

Zenger turned completely around inside the railing, laughing, too excited to know what he was doing. He thumped one of his guards on the shoulder so heartily he almost knocked him down. He tried to shout with

213

the rest but found he had no breath to make any noise. He felt young and happy. He was a different person from the man he had been that morning.

The young judge stared wide-eyed at the sea of waving arms. He was obviously astonished. Thundering with his gavel, he barked out, "Order in the court! Any more applause, and we'll have the leaders of this disturbance jailed for contempt!"

Captain Norris, one of the best-known sea captains of New York and a son-in-law of ex-Judge Morris, strode forward boldly. He was fresh from England, full of sea air, and dressed in the handsomest suit of embroidered cream-colored silk ever seen in New York. Thumping his powerful chest, he roared, "Applause is common in the Supreme Court in London, and was loudest on the acquittal of the seven bishops!"

Everyone remembered the famous trial of the seven bishops for libel, in which the jury had defied the judges. The cheering of the crowd roared up again.

Again Delancey spoke, but no one will ever know what he said, for his decision was completely drowned by the shouts of triumph from the people.

For a moment he sat in glowering rage, watching the men who rushed to congratulate Mr. Hamilton and the prisoner. Then, leaping angrily to his feet, the judge hurried from the room.

Judge Philipse, who had not said a word throughout

the trial, followed him like a dog at his master's heels.

Since Mr. Hamilton limped so pitifully on his sore foot, a dozen shouting, laughing young men picked up his chair with him in it and carried him out. A parade formed and they took him all the way to his tavern.

The sheriff, young Billy Cosby, told the jailor, "I don't know what to do with the prisoner! He can't be released without an order from the judge, and the judge is gone! I guess you'll have to put him back in jail."

So Zenger was dragged away quickly by the two guards and the jailor, a strange climax to a strange trial.

Next morning Zenger's two guards brought him up again to the courtroom. It was almost empty. A Negro slave was wandering among the benches picking up torn and dirty copies of the *Journal*. Another had been sweeping, but they both scurried away when the judges entered.

Zenger found his wife and all six of his children, the chubby Mr. Chambers, who was delighted at the prestige he had gained in this trial, and a few loyal friends. Old Rip Van Dam seemed especially glad to shake Zenger's hand.

Mr. Chambers stood up. "If it please your Honors, in view of the verdict returned yesterday by the trial jury, I humbly move for the discharge of my client from custody."

Judge Delancey sat twitching and fidgeting, evidently thoroughly upset. He was intelligent enough to have understood Mr. Hamilton's speeches, and certainly the astounding behavior of the populace must have driven home any doubts created by the aged attorney's reasoning.

When he opened his mouth to speak, no sound came out, and he had to clear his throat and try again. "Do I hear any objections?" he asked.

The sheriff stood up, looking confused, his hands full of bills. "The jailor tells me these bills are unpaid. They are for food and firewood for the prisoner."

Lewis Morris, Junior, announced promptly, "I'll contribute half the amount, if my friends will supply the balance." He began to pass his hat around, but it did not have to go beyond the old shipbuilder, Van Dam. The small sum was handed to the jailor.

With his youngest son, Freddie, only a year old, carried on one arm and his wife clasping the other, the printer walked slowly, wearily, out into the sunlight for the first time in nine months.

That evening more than forty enthusiastic leaders of the Popular Party entertained Mr. Hamilton at a dinner at the Black Horse Tavern. Their emblem hung proudly on the wall, painted in large letters: "LIBERTY and LAW!"

Several of the gentlemen made speeches, thanking Mr. Hamilton for his masterly, inspiring service to the city and to all mankind. Mr. Hamilton had refused to take any pay for his work.

When he sailed away in Mrs. Alexander's two-masted yacht, the *Journal* reported:

At his departure next day he was saluted with the great guns of several ships in the harbor as a public testimony of the glorious defence he had made in the cause of liberty.

Judge Delancey, feeling that it was his duty to tell his governor the bad news himself, went stiffly down Broadway to the fort. Never before had he walked so slowly. Standing in Cosby's office, he squared his lean shoulders as best he could and gave his message simply.

He waited for Cosby to explode, to swear and shout.

For a long minute the heavy-handed governor slumped in his chair in silence. Now the newspapers would be free to report all his official actions, good and bad. At last he shook himself a little, looked up with eyes empty of hope, and silently reached for the whisky bottle on his desk.

A man cannot live without pride, and his was gone. A few months after the trial he took to his bed, coughing. Winter brought on a fever. While the last snow was melting in the early spring sunlight, Governor Cosby was buried in the chapel in the fort, near the mansion where he had lived in power. With him died an idea—that the government should be run secretly according to the wishes of the officials and that the people should silently accept whatever is done to them —a dangerous, frightening idea, which must never be allowed to live again on American soil.

News came that his friend Judge Harison, the elegant gentleman who had been the mighty recorder of New York, had died of starvation in a poorhouse in London. He must have sold his gold-headed cane and his fine coat with the silver buttons. It is the last scrap of information on record about him. Many of his crimes will never be known. Often they had been written down simply as crimes, for he was powerful enough to prevent his actions from being named. One of the most important elements of freedom of the press has always been the right to tell the people the truth about criminal underlings who have been protected by the governments they have served.

The effect of the trial on Judge Delancey was very deep. He was still young enough to learn. For the next two years he lived almost in hiding, till, at an election for the legislative assembly, he suddenly emerged and got himself voted into it.

Profoundly altered by the Zenger trial, he became a champion of the people's rights and, with his great energy and cleverness, fought vigorous battles in their defense.

Ex-Judge Morris continued to work in London till

the King's officers at last sent a bitter message to Governor Cosby saying that his reasons for having expelled Mr. Morris from the Supreme Court had been insufficient. As an additional proof that Cosby had been wrong, Mr. Morris was appointed by the King to be the first royal governor of New Jersey, which was then separated from New York.

Zenger spent most of his first two weeks of freedom sitting in the sun on his front doorstep, receiving congratulations from a constant stream of fellow townsmen who came to shake his big, square right hand.

As soon as he felt recovered from his sad months in jail, he went on with printing the City Charter, beginning where he had left off a year before. In a few weeks he finished it, delivered six copies to the city aldermen in the same room in which he had been tried, and received seven pounds in payment. It was the handsomest piece of printing he had ever done.

In the *Journal* he soon published all the legal documents concerning his case. Mr. Alexander, eager to make the most of their triumph, helped him collect a word-for-word account of the whole trial, and Zenger printed it. *The Case and Tryal of John Peter Zenger* became the most famous book published in America in his generation. He sold so many copies that he had to print several editions. Two more editions were printed in Boston.

His trial affected the liberties of people in England, also, and five editions of his book were soon printed in London.

Although he continued to publish his *Journal* every Monday, he had learned some caution. Gone were the old slashing, sizzling phrases. But the paper was as bold as ever in stating facts. No governor was again able to do the things Cosby had done.

The legislative assembly rewarded him by having him do the public printing for the colony of New York, when Mr. Bradford was too old to go on with it. Nevertheless Zenger continued to be very poor throughout the remaining eleven years of his life. Altogether he had seven children, and six of them survived to make his last years noisy.

After his death the *Journal* continued to appear. For two years the note at the end of the last page said, "Printed by the Widow Catherine Zenger." She worked hard to make the free press a powerful weapon to protect the lives and liberties of all the people.

Later events showed that her husband's trial had for the first time established freedom of speech and of the press in America. Just as Mr. Hamilton and Attorney General Bradley had quoted previous cases to prove their points, so, from that day on, other lawyers in similar trials have quoted the Zenger case to prove that any newspaper has the right to print the truth about any government officer's official acts.

A son of Lewis Morris, Junior, was named Gouverneur Morris. He became a leading statesman. As he had great literary talent, he was chosen to write the finished version of the Constitution of the United States. And it was he who said, "The trial of Zenger was the germ of American freedom."

A Note from the Author

THE first freedom is the right to speak and print the truth. And America's first great fight for this liberty was the trial of Peter Zenger in 1735, which won freedom of the press both for America and for England.

Although this account has been presented in story form, with details of action fictionalized, the facts stated are true. Not one of these events is imaginary.

This book was written from research in the original papers of Zenger's day, and many of the facts are not in any other book now in print. It is necessary, therefore, to add this appendix, which contains some additional data and samples of the writing published by Zenger.

Zenger was born in 1697 in the western part of Germany called the Palatinate. With his family he fled to the Netherlands, then to England.

His full name was John Peter Zenger, but he usually signed himself J. Peter Zenger. His mother was Hannah Zenger; his brother, John; his sister, Anna Catherine. They came to America in the summer of 1710, the father dying on shipboard.

October 26, 1710, he was apprenticed to Mr. Bradford for eight years. We still have a copy of the indenture which he and his mother and Mr. Bradford signed that day.

New York was soon at war with the French in Canada. In July, 1711, Mr. Bradford earned a little extra money by shoving his apprentice and journeymen into a back attic to make room for some French officers, who were prisoners.

In 1714 Bradford printed a play written by Governor Hunter. And next year he printed a prayer book in the Mohawk Indian language. Zenger must have had a hard time if he set the type for that.

In 1718, when Zenger was twenty-one, he went to Chestertown in Kent County, Maryland, set up a printing shop, married, and became a citizen with the right to vote. In April, 1720, the Maryland Assembly agreed to pay him seven hundred pounds of tobacco for doing their official printing. But his wife died, and apparently he never finished the printing and never received all the tobacco.

A few days after Zenger had left New York, Mr.

Bradford got into trouble with the New York Assembly for not having printed some government documents quickly enough. Next year, in 1719, Bradford tried to cheat the city out of thirty pounds in money. He collected that much to have a new copper plate made for printing paper shillings. Then he used the old plate and did not get a new one at all. But in June the authorities caught him and made him pay back the thirty pounds.

Zenger returned to New York in the spring of 1722 and on September 11 married Anna Catherine Maulin. After that she always signed herself Catherine Zenger. She is famous as probably the inventor of Sunday Schools and certainly one of the first women ever to publish a newspaper. She had most of the management of the *Journal* while Zenger was in jail in 1734 and 1735. Elizabeth Timothy published the South Carolina *Gazette* in 1739, Andrew Bradford's widow the *American Weekly Mercury* in 1742, and Catherine Zenger the New York *Weekly Journal* for two years after her husband's death in 1746.

July 6, 1723, Zenger, Hendrick Michael Cook, and a number of their friends became citizens in New York with the right to vote. They had to apply for this privilege and pay for it. Cook was a weaver and also a musician. Zenger at this time frequently served as a witness when his friends had to sign official documents. Benjamin Franklin's visit to ask Bradford for a job was in October, 1723. Bradford soon made a trip to Philadelphia, where Franklin had some more dealings with him. Apparently he thought Franklin a trouble maker and tried to prevent him from getting a job. Franklin described Bradford as "a cunning old fox," too selfish and slippery to be trusted.

In November, a month after Franklin's visit to New York, Zenger's first child was born and was named John. Next year Mrs. Zenger's sister Ursula married Nick Sijn, and in September, 1725, Zenger's second child, Pieter, was born.

This book tells how Zenger became Mr. Bradford's partner in 1725, quarreled with him over the publishing of New York's first newspaper, and set up a shop of his own on Smith Street in 1726.

In June, 1726, Zenger's brother John, with several friends, became citizens with the right to vote. In September, 1727, Zenger's third child, Nicolas, was born. A few days after the christening Zenger's sister married Fred Bekker. She later had two children, Elizabeth and Frederick, and Zenger was a witness at their baptisms.

Zenger was paid 12 pounds a year for being the organ blower. December 15, 1727, Governor Burnet (whose wife was Dutch) gave a new organ to the Dutch church. Hendrick Michael Cook was appointed on that day to be the organist and to teach Zenger to play.

A few days later Zenger joined with four other Palatines and invested in some land. This was a mistake, for he never made any money out of it.

In 1728 his fourth child, Elizabeth, was born, and in March, 1732, his fifth, Evert.

After Zenger had become organist, the church authorities failed to pay him. In 1732 he played a joke on them by solemnly petitioning for the right to take up a collection from the congregation for his salary. The church fathers saw the point and agreed to pay him.

Governor Cosby arrived that summer, and the *Journal* was started on November 1, 1733. In January, 1734, at the height of the battle between the two newspapers, his sixth child, Frederick, was born. On May 1 he moved to the new shop "on Broad Street near the upper end of the Long Bridge," as his paper described it. On June 18 his brother-in-law Fred Bekker became a citizen with the right to vote, just in time for the hotly contested election of city aldermen.

After that election, all official printing for the city was given to Zenger instead of to Mr. Bradford. Zenger went to jail November 17, 1734, was tried August 4 of the next year, and was let out the following day.

As a reward for his services he was given all official

printing for the colony of New York, beginning in 1737. The following year his old friend Judge Morris, then governor of New Jersey, made him public printer for New Jersey, too.

He also was made one of the tax collectors. However, he lost that job because he was so poor that he spent some of the money he was supposed to hand in. And he soon lost his job of printing city documents, too. The reason given was that he was "an indifferent printer and very ignorant of the English language." This was not true, for his printing, we can see, was at least as good as Mr. Bradford's. But even his friends admitted that he was exasperatingly slow.

In 1738 his seventh child, Catherine, was born.

After the trial Zenger's newspaper began to show unusual skill in the selection and arrangement of its foreign news and literary extracts from English magazines. As Zenger seems to have edited it himself during those eleven years, we have to credit him with real editorial ability.

On July 6, 1746, his daughter Elizabeth married George Cook, a weaver, son of the friend who had taught Zenger to play the organ.

Three weeks later, on July 28, 1746, Zenger died. His friends said that he had been a scholar, for he had known a little Latin and could write good humorous poetry in English. Judge Delancey, on the other hand, had called him "a dull, thick-headed fellow," who "had a knack of rhyming."

Zenger's eldest son, John, had married in 1741. He had three children, quarreled with his mother, and became a printer. Judging by some things he wrote, he had the same direct, homely quality as his father had, and the same humor, though with a touch of bitterness added. He died in 1751, the same year that Zenger's second son, Pieter, was married.

William Bradford was born in England in 1663. He was apprenticed to a printer, Mr. Sowle. He married his master's daughter, Elizabeth.

He was sent to America by George Fox, the Quaker leader, in 1685, and settled in Philadelphia. But he soon quarreled with the Quakers because he tried to reform their religion, and was scolded several times by the authorities. He even ran off to England in a huff, but returned immediately. In 1692, when he was twenty-nine, he was arrested and tried, as told in this book, and was sent to New York the following year.

In New York he printed books in English, Dutch, and French, mostly almanacs and religious works. He printed the government's official reports, and also paper money. In 1724 he began a paper mill in New Jersey.

In 1731 his wife died. May 17, 1733, his apprentice

James Parker, then nineteen years old, ran away, stealing some books, knives, printer's tools, and also a number of pairs of fancy stockings, some silk and some wool, that Bradford was selling in his shop. Bradford advertised twenty shillings reward to anyone who would capture him. But after a while the boy came back of his own free will and patched up the quarrel with his master.

In 1734, at the height of the battle between his newspaper and Zenger's, Bradford married a widow, Cornelia Smith, and moved to another house on Hanover Square.

He retired in 1742 and died ten years later, aged eighty-nine.

His son Andrew became a citizen with the right to vote in 1708, two years before Zenger arrived in America. When Zenger entered their house in 1710 Andrew was old Mr. Bradford's partner. Two years later Andrew went to Philadelphia and set up a shop of his own. In 1719 he began a newspaper, the *American Weekly Mercury* (also called the *American Weekly Messenger*).

He did all the official printing for the government of Pennsylvania for about ten years.

He had plenty of trouble. In 1722 he was summoned before the Council of Pennsylvania and scolded for having printed unwelcome advice to the legislative assembly. The governor issued an order to him "that he must not for the future presume to publish anything relating to or concerning the affairs of this government or the government of any other of his Majesty's colonies, without the permission of the Governor or Secretary of this province."

Not being a fool, Andrew Bradford apologized, of course. But if he and other printers had obeyed that outrageous, tyrannous, and barbaric order, the whole press of America would have been gagged and useless.

Fortunately he had courage. On February 26, 1723, he published a strong criticism of the Massachusetts authorities for their action against James Franklin (mentioned in this book in Chapter Five), calling them "bigots, hypocrites, and tyrants."

A few years later he published a series of essays called the "Busy-Body Papers," written by Benjamin Franklin and others. One of these articles, for liberty and against hereditary power, written by a friend of Zenger's, the Reverend Dr. Alexander Campbell of Long Island, alarmed the Pennsylvania authorities, and they arrested Andrew Bradford and sent him to jail.

However, he talked his way out, and they let him go without a trial. Perhaps they thought they had scared him. If so, they were soon disappointed, for from then on his newspaper was bolder than ever, publishing many of the strongest essays in favor of political liberty.

However, Benjamin Franklin immediately began to run a rival newspaper. And in 1730, the year after Andrew Bradford's arrest, Franklin got the official government printing away from him.

Old Mr. Bradford's other son, William, Junior, would not be a printer. He went away to sea. However, he married a Dutch woman, rented a house near his father's printing shop in New York, and had two sons. One of these, William Bradford III, was adopted by Andrew Bradford in Philadelphia and later became one of the boldest publishers supporting the American Revolution.

James Parker and Henry de Foreest, the two boys apprenticed to Mr. Bradford in 1725 in time for the beginning of his newspaper, later became famous printers. They were both such liars that we cannot depend on any of the things they wrote about Mr. Bradford or Zenger.

How did William Cosby become governor?

When Cosby was governor of Minorca, the people objected because he spent the government's money on himself. He quarreled with a Spanish merchant, took from him a large quantity of snuff, and sold it for nine thousand pounds sterling. The officials in London, on complaint from the people, called him home. On the way, he foolishly spent his loot making a triumphal tour across Europe.

In London he was tried, was found guilty, and was ordered to pay back the money or go to jail. Having spent it, he could not pay it back.

But he had powerful friends, the Duke of Grafton and the Duke of Newcastle, and he had married Grace Montagu, a sister of the second Earl of Halifax. As these men did not want to let him go to jail, they loaned him ten thousand pounds, most of which he had to hand over to the court immediately.

These friends then deliberately had him appointed governor of New York and New Jersey so that he could get money quickly and pay it back to them.

He began to do this at once. He bought all new uniforms and equipment for the soldiers in New York, paid for them at English prices, charged the British government for them at New York prices, which were twice as high, and pocketed the difference. He also collected money "for gifts for the Indians." Arriving in New York, he persuaded the New York legislative assembly to give him a reward for his supposed services in their behalf before he had left London. They voted him 750 pounds, but he swore and shouted and bullied them into raising it to one thousand pounds.

By these means he collected over 8,000 pounds for

the time before his arrival in America. But as this **was** not enough to pay off his debt, he was not satisfied.

He had asked the King to let him have half of Van Dam's salary, too. Shortly after his arrival he presented this demand and tried to make Van Dam pay.

This was very foolish, because the King's order was worded in such a way that Cosby and Van Dam were to split fifty-fifty all that both of them had received before Cosby's arrival in New York. So when Cosby asked Van Dam for nine hundred pounds, Van Dam paid a friend in London to do some research for him. Zenger printed the result: Cosby owed Van Dam more than three thousand five hundred pounds. There the matter ended, for Zenger's pamphlets made it impossible for Cosby to go on trying to rob Van Dam.

James Alexander was born in Scotland in 1691. He studied science. In 1715 he went as army engineer with a Scottish army to fight the English. When a much larger English army came to meet them, however, the Scots thought better of the idea and returned home, but some were caught and punished.

Young Alexander took refuge in Devon with his cousin, Henry, fifth Earl of Stirling, who arranged for him to go to America that same year. On shipboard he met William Smith, later his partner.

Mr. Alexander became a surveyor in New Jersey and

was appointed recorder (that is, judge of the criminal court) in Perth Amboy. He soon held various other political offices, including that of a member of his Majesty's Council for New York.

In 1721 he married Polly Spratt, widow of a Dutch merchant, Mr. Provoost. As a girl she had sailed a boat in summer, had gone ice skating in winter, and was noted for having been able to slide down hill standing up on a sled on a steeper hill than the boys could do it on. She spoke Dutch as often as English and could converse with the Indians in their own language.

She continued to run her first husband's business, importing and exporting, mostly cloth and flour, while Mr. Alexander studied law and became New York's outstanding lawyer.

He kept up his interest in science, too, and corresponded with leading scientists in England and Europe, including the famous astronomer Halley.

Mr. and Mrs. Alexander had at least nine children.

It is a curious fact that his ancestor, Sir William Alexander, Earl of Stirling (1580–1640), a poet, was given Canada (all of it) as a gift by Charles I in 1621.

In 1747 James Alexander became heir to the title, but did not bother to do anything about it.

After his death in 1756 his son William (born in 1726) went to Great Britain to claim the title. His right to use it was accepted in Scotland, though not in England. Later, known as Lord Stirling, he served as a general under George Washington in the American Revolution and lost one important battle.

This book tells how James Alexander and his partner William Smith were expelled from the New York bar in their attempt to defend Zenger. They argued before a committee of the legislative assembly that the judges' order expelling them was illegal.

Two years later (in 1737) the same judges admitted that it had been illegal, and the lawyers returned to their jobs. But those were two long years for them. Mr. Alexander helped his wife run her shop, but Mr. Smith had no way to support his large family.

Their attempt to free the judges had failed. For another forty years American judges continued to be appointed by the King's governor "during our will and pleasure." So they continued to be under the governors' orders. The people of America often suffered from cruel and unjust judges during that time.

Years later the legislative assembly refused to pay the salaries of judges appointed during the governor's will and pleasure. The royal government in London replied by collecting a special tax from the people of New York with which to pay the judges. The fight grew fiercer.

Because the attempt to free them had failed in Zenger's trial, it became one of the major causes of the American Revolution. In 1776 the Declaration of Independence accused King George III: "He has made judges dependent on his will alone for the tenure of their offices and the amount and payment of their salaries."

At last the freedom of American judges was won by the shedding of blood.

John Chambers, the lawyer whom Zenger did not at first trust, was active in business in New York as early as 1722, began practicing law in 1725, and several times was rewarded for serving the city. When William Smith founded what was probably New York's first bar association of lawyers July 28, 1729, Mr. Chambers was one of the members. That autumn he became an alderman and served until voted out in the hotly contested election of 1734, when Zenger printed a handbill against him.

He was wealthy enough to lend money to the city on one occasion, and was a vestryman of Trinity Church, as Mr. Bradford had been. Owning a fine house on Broadway, he joined with two neighbors in the famous deal over part of the parade ground. These three gentlemen in March, 1733, signed a lease whereby they would rent the land from the city at one peppercorn a year for eleven years. At their own expense they were to build a fence around the little field at the end of Broadway near the fort, ". . . to make a Bowling Green thereof, with walks therein, for the beauty and ornament of said street, as well as for the recreation and delight of the inhabitants of the city."

It was New York's first park. Mr. Chambers and his two neighbors probably made a small profit by collecting a penny from each man who bowled on the green. That is how the place got its name, and it is still called Bowling Green.

Mr. Chambers was related by marriage to Judge James Delancey, but the relationship was a little complicated. Mr. Chambers' wife, Anne Van Courtlandt, was a cousin of another Anne Van Courtlandt, who was the young judge's mother.

Mr. Chambers must have felt odd standing in court between Judge Delancey and Mr. Alexander, for Mrs. Chambers was also a cousin to Mrs. Alexander.

After the Zenger trial Mr. Chambers was very successful. In 1754 he became a member of his Majesty's Council, in 1756 a judge of the Supreme Court, and later chief justice. He died in 1765.

Francis Harison, writing in the *Gazette* for April 1, 1734, guessed the principal contributors to Zenger's paper and named them thus: 1, Amsterdam Crane; 2, Connecticut Mastif; 3, Philip Baboon, Sr.; 4, Philip

Baboon, Jr.; 5, Sythian Unicorn; 6, Wild Peter from the Banks of the Rhine.

These were: 1, Rip Van Dam; 2, William Smith; 3, Lewis Morris, ex-chief justice; 4, Lewis Morris, Junior; 5, James Alexander; 6, Zenger.

From Zenger's *Journal* for November 12, 1733:

Some Governors may certainly err, misbehave, and become criminal. It is this therefore which makes the liberty of the press necessary, for if such an overgrown criminal or an impudent monster in iniquity cannot immediately be caught by ordinary legal justice, let him yet receive the lash of satire. Let the glaring truths of his ill administration if possible awaken his conscience, and if he has no conscience, arouse his fear. These methods may in time, by watching and exposing his actions, make him at least more cautious, and perhaps at last bring down the great haughty criminal within the reach and grasp of ordinary justice. This advantage of exposing the crimes of wicked officers of the government makes the liberty of the press necessary. Liberty of the press is a curb, a bridle, a terror, a shame, and restraint to evil governors.

From Zenger's *Journal* for November 19, 1733:

No nation ever lost the liberty of freely speaking, writing, or publishing, but immediately lost all their liberties and became slaves. Anyone who is against freedom of the press is an enemy to his country.

Zenger and the leaders of the Popular Party were fighting for the right of newspapers to report the governor's official actions. But in their excitement they sometimes went further and printed comments on Cosby's red coat and even his teeth. They called him "an old baboon."

The baboon is of a reddish color, chatters extremely, and no person is in danger of being bit by him, for he has lost his fore teeth. Some persons in the country propose to have a large wooden cage made, and do not doubt of getting much money by showing him.

The *Journal* violently attacked Cosby's habit of swearing (not printing the real words he used):

Shall a fellow that is but one degree removed from an idiot, with a full-mouthed 'Sacrament, Donder, and Blixum!' dispose of us and our properties as he pleases? As if a noisy tongue in the empty head of a creature that has nothing human but the shape, was the fittest engine to govern with!"

Francis Harison wrote some lavish praises of Governor Cosby and dropped them in the *Gazette* for November 5, 1733. He wrote of the "blessings which we enjoy under a government greatly envied," and, describing a dinner party at the governor's mansion, wrote, "The easy manner, order, and admirable address which appeared through the whole, rendered this the most agreeable night that has been known here."

Zenger replied by printing the following description of Judge Harison:

A large spaniel, of about five foot five inches high, has lately strayed from his kennel with his mouth full of fulsome praises and in his ramble dropped them in the *New York Gazette*. When a puppy he was marked thus: F H, and a cross in his forehead. But the mark being worn out, he has taken upon him in a heathenish manner to abuse mankind by imposing a great many gross falsehoods upon them. Whoever will strip the said praises of all their fulsomeness and send the beast back to his kennel, shall have the thanks of all honest men, and all reasonable charges.

This produced a great deal of laughter in the taverns, but for a while Harison wrote nothing more in the *Gazette*. Soon the *Journal* commented on his silence:

The spaniel strayed away is of his own accord returned to his kennel, from whence he begs leave to assure the public that all those fulsome praises were dropped in the *New York Gazette* by the express orders of his master. That for the gross falsehoods he is charged with imposing upon mankind, he is willing to undergo any punishment the people will impose on him, if they can make full proof in any court of record that any one individual person in this province, that knew him, believed any of them.

Zenger's own book, *The Case and Tryal of John Peter Zenger,* has been reprinted so often that it can still be bought and is in most large libraries. It consists of a number of the documents about the burning of his papers and about his arrest, and a word-for-word transcription of large parts of his trial.

Here is a little of Andrew Hamilton's magnificent speech to the jury:

Gentlemen, this is a reign of liberty, and while men keep within the bounds of truth, I hope they may with safety speak and write their opinions of the conduct of men in power—I mean of that part of their conduct only which affects the liberty or property of the people under their administration. Were this to be denied, then the next step may make us slaves! For what can slavery be but this—to suffer the greatest injuries and oppressions without the liberty of complaining?

The loss of liberty, to a generous mind, is worse than death. And yet we know there have been those in all ages who for the sake of their own advancement or for some imaginary honor, have freely lent a helping hand to oppress, nay, to destroy their country. This brings to mind that saying of the immortal Brutus, when he looked upon Caesar's appointees, who were very powerful men, but by no means good men. "You Romans," said Brutus, "if I may still call you so, consider what you are doing! Remember that you are assisting Caesar to forge those very chains which one day he will make yourselves wear!"

I am truly very unequal to such an undertaking as this.

241

PETER ZENGER

You see I labor under the weight of many years and am
borne down with great infirmities of body. Yet, old and
weak as I am, I should think it my duty, if required, to go
to the utmost parts of the land where my service could be
of any use in assisting to quench the flame of prosecutions
set on foot by the government to deprive a people of the
right of complaining against the arbitrary attempts of men
in power!

But to conclude: the question before the court and you,
gentlemen of the jury, is not of small nor private concern.
It is not the cause of the poor printer, nor of New York
alone, which you are now trying. No! It may in its consequences affect every freeman in America. It is the best
cause. It is the cause of Liberty!

I make no doubt but your upright conduct this day will
not only entitle you to the love and esteem of your fellow
citizens; but everyone who prefers freedom to a life of
slavery will bless and honor you, as men who have baffled
the attempt of tyranny and by an impartial and uncorrupt
verdict have laid a noble foundation for securing to ourselves, our neighbors, and our children, that to which
nature and the laws of our country have given us a right:
the liberty of exposing and opposing arbitrary power, by
speaking and writing truth!"